FAQ ME

JAMES ALTUCHER

James Altucher
FAQ ME

ISBN-13: 978-1479256563

www.jamesaltucher.com

Cover design and layout idea by Dominic Rivera

Cover picture by Claudia Azula Altucher
www.ClaudiaYoga.com

Design, Layout, and Typesetting by Alexander Becker
www.alexanderbecker.net

Contents

Dedication

To Claudia, Josie, Mollie. I ask them questions every day and always forget to write the answers down.

And a special thank you to all of you who asked questions in Twitter.

About The Author

James Altucher has failed at numerous business and careers and succeeded at a few of them. He has loved and lost and loved again. He has tried over and over to... [insert just about anything from chess to poker to hula hooping to massive lifestyle experimentation]. He has won success and lost it and occasionally wins it again. Has been on a quest for the meaning of happiness since the age of six (only because before that, happiness was fairly easy and simple). He has written eight prior books including "I Was Blind But Now I See."

James writes at jamesaltucher.com the most personal, embarrassing stuff a person can possibly write. He tweets @jaltucher.

FAQ ME

WHY WOULD ANYONE ASK ME?

I've failed at just about everything I've done. I've lost tens of millions of dollars after making it from scratch. I've been divorced. As a father, you can make your own judgments based on what I've written. As an entrepreneur I've had successes and failures. I've fought addictions, some of them I've won, some I would say are still in process. Yet, people ask me questions.

I've been an entrepreneur and writer for the past 15 years. About a year and a half ago, I started blogging. The main component of my blog was that I would be honest and revealing. The times when I would be on the floor and just struggling to get up and get motivated. The times when I would pray for nothing but my own death so at least life insurance could be used to keep my kids happy. That's how stupid I was. That is how revealing I was on my blog. And then some.

People were emailing me many questions, *"How did you get yourself off the floor?" "What do you think of X?" "How can I build Y?" "How do I come up with ideas?" "How can I self-publish a book?" "How can I be happy when I'm going through a divorce?"*

I am not very good at answering emails. However, I wanted to answer these questions, and I felt that not just me but anyone can answer the questions. So I started to schedule one hour a week, Thursdays from 3:30-4:30 EST, so anyone could ask. I would Tweet answers away, but really, anyone could. That is what's great about Twitter.

And why would I want to do this? What good does it do me? Really... nothing. But I love it. I used to religiously read the advice column "Dear Abby's column" as a kid. Then I would buy the collected columns (since she had decades worth of material) when they came out in book form. She had been doing it since 1956 and her daughter continues the tradition. And then there was "Ask Ann Landers" which was every bit as good and done by her twin sister. Of course, they couldn't use their real names. "Ann Landers" real name was "Eppie Lederer." I fantasized they were related to me (my great grandfather's last name was "Lederer").

People would ask them anything. I remember one in particular. A woman followed her husband late at night to a strip club. The man went in the back with a woman. Later, under interrogation from the wife he claimed, *"all I got were sexual favors."* In other words, he was trying to say, no big deal. This girl wanted to know (from Abby, or Ann, I forget which) if this was okay.

I forget their response. But right then and there I decided I wanted to be just like "Dear Abby." I wanted people to feel comfortable asking me about "sexual favors." What could be more fun in life?

Initially I majored in Psychology at college. My dad asked me, *"Why do you want to major in Psychology? Psychologists don't make any money. Then you won't meet any girls."*

"But what if I don't want to meet the kind of girl who is going to like me just because I have money."

"She's not going to like you because you have money," my dad in his infinite logic was trying to explain. *"She's going to like you because you are the KIND OF GUY who can make money."*

He did not convince me. Unfortunately, some bad things happened along the way towards me being a professional clinical psychologist – not – and future Dear Abby.

Psychology 101 was considered a "gut class." 2000 people were in the class. The teacher gave the same multiple choice exams every year and there were only 2 tests and a final, and that was your entire grade. I read every psychology book in the library. I was passionate about the topic. I got a D– in the class.

I don't really know how I got a D–. I studied. I took notes. I attended every class (the only time I did that during my entire college education). I also knew people were cheating (studying the prior year's multiple choice exams, knowing they would be the same). But I assumed I would be great at multiple choice exams.

Well, somehow I wasn't. I don't even know what went wrong. They never handed the tests back.

I figured, OK, no problem. I'll take Social Psychology, which was the next class higher. Unfortunately, by this point I really had stopped attending classes. Then one day I attended a class and there was a "pop midterm." I had never even heard of such a thing. But my entire grade was going to be determined by this midterm (and then there would be one more test – the final) that I had not studied for, prepared for, took notes for, in any way.

I pulled off a C+. Then I went to see a guidance counselor to determine what I should major in.

"Well," she said, *"one thing is for sure. The only major you CAN'T major in is psychology."*

"But I want to be a psychologist," I told her.

She raised her eyebrows. *"I think that's not going to be so easy for you."* And hence my feelings about college education began to form. What a load of—

I don't have all the answers. I do not admit that I do. In fact, if you were to just superficially look at the chronological history of my life you would see it mostly filled with miserable failures punctuated by the occasional success. I've lost millions of dollars at different points. I'm a divorced father of two. I was thrown out of graduate school. I've failed at many businesses.

During the hour I answer questions, people know that I work hard to give the best answer I can, and I hope the answers are occasionally helpful. Then, I expand some of the answers into blog posts and other people provide answers in the comments as well.

WHAT IS NEW IN THIS BOOK:

For this book, I've picked out the best questions and answers, expanded further, and categorized by subject. There's a lot of original material for many of the questions.

I also added some Q&A that was asked privately via emails (while keeping identities private). This is all original material in the book.

I hope you like the book and that it's helpful to you. I also hope you join me for more Twitter Q&As on Thursdays.

PURPOSE OF LIFE

What do you do when things keep getting worse?

Around the summer of 2000 I lost a lot of money. About a million dollars a week, in cash. This may seem like, *"ok, at least he had that money and he must have stopped before he went to zero."* But I went to zero.

The worst part was finding the strength to continue going. Staring at the screen, mumbling about fate, and all those stupid decisions, suddenly all the cruelty and malice in the world that had been storing up just for me was unleashed for the first time in my thirty years of life and it wouldn't let me go.

I went from having more money than I knew what to do with to having zero. I could have given money to charity. I could have set up my kids for life. I could have used the money to help my father when he was sick. I could have saved his life. I could have saved my life.

I could have saved myself from losing my apartment. I could have saved myself from so many sleepless nights. I never slept. At most, two hours in a stretch. And I would drink every night. I would sit snug in this giant couch inside this giant apartment in the dark thinking, *"how stupid was I? I made money when it was easy and then I lost it all. Now I'm never going to make it back again and my kids and everyone else around me will suffer. I've done bad things to people and this was karma. I've squandered all the good will I created as a kid."*

I honestly thought that the success I had was generated as a combination of luck and because I spent many years meditating as a kid. I thought that I had built up some karmic warchest and I used it to generate enough money to dominate the world and then I squandered it. Now I was gone. But I couldn't kill myself because I had two kids to pay for. I had to make sure they were ok.

I went to therapists, astrologers, psychics, Zen teachers, Zen therapists. One psychic said I needed to find a coconut TODAY and smash into the street. At 10pm one night I decided to do it. I had two problems: where to get the coconut at 10 p.m., and how to find an empty street in Manhattan to smash it.

I went out and around the corner where there was a Thai restaurant. I figured they must have a coconut. They didn't really understand me. Finally one waiter did. He started speaking in Thai to a woman who I assumed was his mother. *"No coconut,"* she said, but she wrote down an address where I could find one.

Then, behind me I heard, *"James, what are you doing here?"*

It was Flash. I had been playing chess with him for 15 years in Washington Square Park. I didn't know this but apparently at night the entire Washington Square Park crowd moved to this Thai restaurant on the corner of Reade and Church, a few blocks from the World Trade Center. Flash owed me money but I knew I would never collect it.

Instead I played chess for a few hours. JP was there also. *"Why are you out right now?"* he said, *"I have to find a coconut and smash it into the street."* He laughed and said, *"I knew it. There must be a woman involved."* And we all laughed and played chess. A small respite for me in a five year period of non-stop pain and agony.

Then I went to the address the woman gave me. It was a basement store in the lower east side that was still open at 11 p.m. I told them I needed a coconut. A guy came back with this hairy round brown thing. I bought it. Then I wandered up and down Washington Street until I was sure nobody was looking. I threw down the coconut as hard as I could. It smashed everywhere, the milk splattering my pants and everything around.

Things are going to change now, I thought. Sort of like that line from the Beck song, *"Loser:" "things are going to change. I can feel it."*

Things did change. I lost my job as a venture capitalist. That job was at least paying my mortgage. I got kicked off the board of a company I started. Selling that company was my last hope. I was too demoralized to stop it or to start anything new. I would lie around, unable to get myself back up and start generating new ideas.

I tried to get a loan. Nobody would lend to me. Not even when I paraded two little babies to the bank. Banks have rules, you know. No lending to degenerates. At least not yet. That was years later when banks would lend to anyone.

Every month I'd go to the ATM machine and I'd have this feeling like someone was stabbing me all over my body and mind when I looked at how much was left in the account. I'd yell at my now ex-wife as if it were her fault, *"How are we supposed to live on this. We are GOING TO ZERO!"*

And because I kept saying it over and over, the reality was created and we did go to zero. "The Law of Attraction" works in reverse much more than it works in a positive way.

Then 9/11 happened. I hate talking about 9/11. So many people had it far worse than me on that day. Far, far, worse. I was standing on Church Street when the first plane flew overhead. Dan said to me, *"Is the President coming into town today?"* because the plane was so low. It was right over us. Even though it was actually about 600 feet higher, everyone on the street felt they had to duck because we had never seen a plane that low coming in so fast and we all watched it go into the building.

After that there was no way I could sell my apartment, with the mortgage each month that was crushing me. The week after 9/11 I decided to be brave and buy the stock market as it opened. This is how I went to zero. I lost basically whatever I had left. I finally couldn't take it anymore. On Friday of that week at around 10:30 I had to sell everything. I was screaming at my broker on the phone, *"I'm going to go broke!"* And he sold whatever I had left. Scraps that I knew I could use to pay my mortgage a few months more. Starting around a minute later the stock market went on a run upwards that lasted at least three months. If I had held on for at least 5 more hours I would've doubled my money on the week. If I had held on for 3 more months I would've had more money than ever. Instead I was broke.

It took another year to sell. I started missing payments. I couldn't afford diapers. I got shit all over my head.

Nobody would return my calls. I asked my neighbor if a bank or a hedge fund would hire me. He said, *"typically you have to have a track record that's good."* And I was too ashamed to ask him more. I actually had no skills I could think of that could pay my expenses. Dot-com entrepreneurs were a dime a dozen and everyone was broke after the bust. No bankers or VCs would return my phone calls. There was nobody for me to sue. It was my entire fault and I'm not a litigious person anyway.

One time I called my parents. I needed to borrow $1000. That's all. After having millions. It was 14 months after 9/11. I finally had sold my place but the deal had not yet closed and I had no money. I needed money to move. To live.

They began to yell at me. They didn't want to lend me the money. I hung up the phone. I didn't talk to them for six months. Then my dad had a stroke and that's the next time I talked to them, although he never woke up from his stroke. So the last time I spoke to him I had hung up on him.

Everyone says that *"things cycle"* or *"what goes down, goes up."* But that's not true. My dad was in his stroke-coma for three years. He never got better. He got steadily worse and worse. They would drop his body on the floor when moving him from one institution to the next. He had bed sores so bad you could see through to the skeleton. My family thought I didn't visit him enough. But I was scared and didn't want to be even more depressed and I had my own two kids to take care of.

I stayed in my new house all the time, about sixty miles north of the city. I gained about 20 lbs because I was no longer pacing the streets of Manhattan at all hours of the night and there was blizzard after blizzard where I lived. I was in exile and I had no idea what would happen. For the first year after I moved into town I didn't speak with anyone. I didn't want to. This was only temporary, I thought.

The worst part was trying to find the strength to continue. So my projects turned to zero. What was the point. Day after day. All the music I had danced to just a few years earlier was now silenced. The jukebox was broken. The dance hall was closed. Every night I woke up in dread, terrified of yet one more insecure tomorrow. I wasn't even brave enough to kill myself. And the truth was only leading me closer to a death agony. The agony that youth was gone, and for the rest of my tomorrows I was finished, crushed by my responsibilities, and the carved out hole of loss inside of me.

I went into one store and asked the woman behind the counter, *"is it just me or does the entire world seem like it's depressed, as if people can't shake the utter sadness of just being alive?"* She looked at me and said, *"Do you know anything about computers? I can't get my computer to work."*

A close relative of mine wrote me, *"You weren't even as good as your father. He never would've lost a house that his children loved and been such a disappointment like you were."* The few times I would venture into the city I couldn't think of a single friend or family member I could call that I could spend time with and who would want to see me and we'd all be happy and just enjoy. I had nothing and nobody. And I'm not blaming them. It was my entire fault.

I'm still afraid of slipping back into that crevice. The Earth shakes every few years. 2008, for instance. Cracks in the Earth open. Bridges that were secure for 50 years break and cars fall into the water. Once you've seen the darkness in the center of the Earth, the heat that can burn your brain to cinders, you know it's always there, an open invitation to come back to it. I knew too much, but not enough to ever come back. Once the bridge cracks, the car is already doomed.

I can tell you it all came back. I can say, *"that's why I'm writing this."* I can say, *"don't worry, things do cycle if you picture it and let it."* But things don't always come back. Sometimes things get worse and worse.

The important thing is that right around the middle of all of this, I started planting seeds. The abominable pressure of being forced to live, forced me to plant tiny seeds. Life goes on, the future is a joke, but we can never forget it exists and its hungry and it's waiting to eat and destroy us so we must have food to give it. I was planting a garden. You pull up weeds. You dig out the dirt. You put seeds in, you lay excrement over it. Some plants get eaten up by ravenous birds. But some seeds are left alone and, if cared for, are allowed to blossom. That's why I'm still alive. Because of the seeds planted. In retrospect I wish I had planted more of them but it's ok.

I planted new seeds every day. I still do.

Maybe I can also lie to myself and say I am a better person for having been through things. Maybe I came through the other side and there was more light on this side than the side I started on. I don't know. I hope so. Some seeds I planted ten years ago are still growing. Still need to be harvested.

The key is to plant the seeds. And never stop, even if weather, even if animals, even if mutations, look as if they are going to damage the garden and destroy it. Seeds take time to grow. A long time. And they need to be loved with patience, just like children. And there are seeds designed for every season. The key is to go out there, dig up dirt, and plant. Every day.

You don't know what the final outcome might be. What the DNA of each seed holds for your garden. But over time, over years, over a lifetime, the garden turns lush – there are colors, there is food to eat, there are perennials that, like old friends, always return every year when the cold is over. You can never ever stop planting the seeds. Every day. Eventually there is a thick patch of joy where there was once nothing but dirt, weeds, and mud.

And you can look at it and finally say, *"This is me. I did this."* What seed will you plant today?

What do you think is the purpose of life? @adriennetran

"Purpose" is somewhere in the middle of *"having everything you want"* and "wanting nothing."

We have to feed our families, we have to be responsible, we can't just hide in a cave (i.e. want nothing) but at some point there needs to be room to develop the soul.

So if we get everything we want, but we want as little as possible, somewhere in that spectrum lies our true purpose to be found.

I try every day to throw things out. I've accumulated a lot in the past 40 years. I try to simplify. I also try to simplify my relationships. Attend fewer meetings. Learn more during the extra quiet periods I have. By doing this I can learn more about what my passions might be, how to pursue them, how to enjoy them. Or worse cast, I avoid being around people and situations that dissuade me from purpose.

On a grander scale, I think all purpose is spiritual in nature. Not spiritual in a religious sense. But in *"something else."* All of the atoms in my body were ultimately created in the Big Bang. All information in my brain comes from events that happened after that one moment. I think ultimate purpose is connecting with those gaps in between the atoms, in between those units of micro-information that may have existed before the first moments of the Universe.

I know that sounds a little crazy. But if I believe anything at all, I believe that that's possible.

DATING

What are your feelings concerning online dating? Would you treat it like a new business, considering the interactions?
@jeehtoven

To make online dating work for you, you have to treat it as if it were almost a fulltime job. When I first started dating after the divorce, every evening, if I was not out on a date, I was signing up for online dating services, sending or responding to over 20 emails a night. I was making phone calls (after "chatting" through the service since sometimes people want to hear you on the phone to make sure there's not a wife standing right there).

I became so proficient about the good and bad features that I started my own online dating service called *140love.com*. Unfortunately, that venture did not work. The basic idea was that not only would you get matched to someone but you could quickly decide if you liked their personality based on their profiles as well as their tweets.

The problem with the service was that many Twitter accounts are not anonymous. Nobody wanted to sign up for a non-anonymous online dating site.

So I was online 3-4 hours a night sending out messages to profiles I liked. I spent an hour filling out the eHarmony form and only at the end they told me I wasn't qualified *("Our research shows that people who are separated usually do not have relationships that work out.")*

I cut losses very quickly. If a conversation started that I felt was going nowhere, I stopped it. If a date happened and I sensed it was not going to work out, I cut it short and that was that. Even if I felt like things could move forward, if I didn't think it would end in a long-term relationship, I stopped it.

I had very clear goals. I wanted to fall in love. I wanted someone to fall in love with me. I didn't want any games where we had to pretend to not love each other while we slowly eased into it. I work pretty fast. I wasn't a believer in "the Rules" and whenever I felt I was being sucked into that game, I would back out.

Nor did I lead anyone on. For me, there was no point in just going on dates if I knew the relationship was not going to be long-term. Everything you do in life, good or bad, has consequences. The most obvious consequence of having sex with someone you don't want to have a long-term relationship with is that you could hurt that person's feelings AND, that could've been the night you would have met the love of your life if only you had been home sending messages out.

The one thing I will say is: get used to tons of rejection. Maybe 10:1 on rejections no matter how good you are (unless you are a beautiful woman, then the ratio is probably reverse).

For me it was work. Every day sending messages. Every day trying different services. And then the actual dates. I made the mistake of arranging dinners with everyone. Claudia, who became my wife, had a better method. I met her through an online dating service.

On her profile she said she was from Buenos Aires. I wrote her a first message saying, *"I always wanted to visit Brazil."*

She wrote back saying, *"That's great but Buenos Aires is in Argentina."* So I thought I blew it. But she suggested meeting for a cup of tea. I pushed for dinner. Who knew what could happen?

"No," she said. *"Tea."* She had it right. A tea could be just fifteen minutes. A dinner is two hours and two hundred dollars (at least the way I was drinking back then it was).

And so we met for tea. And now we're married.

Do you have any dating advice for introverts? @dylanized

Yes. If you spend even one night at home, you are in trouble. As Gretzky says, *"skate to where the puck is going, not where it's at."*

So... go to tango classes. Go to yoga. Go to cooking classes. Join book clubs. Don't think you'll go to one tango class and meet the love of your life. All of these things are seeds that you plant. Some of the seeds will grow, some will not.

If you find yourself with free time after this, sign up for every dating service. Send out twenty notes a day. Vary them up. Make them funny, clever. I would do it for you but I would have to charge. I was a dating service expert. I used all of them.

And remember that you have to handle rejection, lots of it. But even a rejection is a seed planted. It builds strength in you and gets the word out: you are looking, you are available.

Most importantly, go to all the places where there are more women than men. Believe me! Women want to meet you just as much as you want to meet them. And they love introverts.

Look at me! I'm hideous. But I worked it, and it worked.

I want a relationship with someone who is actually like me. So what is the next step? I'm in school until summer next year, which means I can't go anywhere.
@spekkhogger123

Let me ask you a couple of questions:

- Can you join a church choir?
- Are there any tango classes in a 30 mile radius?
- There are definitely yoga or Pilates classes
- Go to the library and see if there are any book groups you can join
- Are there any 12-step meetings in your area? (they are not as bad as you think). Like "business owners debtors anonymous" for instance?
- Cooking classes?

And so on.

Find what classes or groups are in a 30 mile radius that, statistically speaking, are made up of mostly women. That's the next step.

The step after that is going to one of those things.

Note to self: idea for a business: build a search engine that will tell me within 30 miles of me where all the classes are that have a 10:1 female to male ratio.

At what moment did you know you were in love? Did you have a Shazam moment!?!
@martycos

I'm a first date fall-in-love kind of guy. So after our first date with Claudia we sat down on a bench in Tompkins Square Park and said nothing. I didn't feel awkward about it. That's when I knew I was in love. No Shazam moment. I knew I could be comfortable with this person. [See, "How I Met Claudia"[1]]. It was such a relief from all the other experiences I had been having.

How do you know if you are in love or just limerice?
@RolandBarat

This is another way of saying you don't know right now. You just met the girl. You're having sex. You love her unique smile – unique from every other smile you've ever been given. She gets you to do things you never thought about doing before. She gets you to laugh. She gets you to daydream about what life would be like with her, and you hate the thought of life without her.

I get it. We've all been there. Done that. And then it doesn't work out.

That's okay. Most things don't work out. But we're not in tomorrow.

Always ask yourself: What am I going to do today. Today is the only day that matters.

So ask this today and be honest:

- Do you want the same thing out of a relationship (presumably, if you love her, you want a long-term committed relationship)

1 http://bit.ly/mDC2uD

- Do you both have similar values about friendships, places you want to live, luxuries you want to have (or not)

- Do you like the way she treats you and is sensitive to what you want?

Ask these questions every day. If the answer comes up "no" then talk about it with her. Being with someone forever (getting married) means you want to spend 50 years with a person. That's never happened before in history but it's happening now because of longer life spans.

So you need to ask those questions every day. And for that day, and that day only, you know.

Suppose you've gone on three or four dates with a girl, do you ever ask her: Where do we stand?
@eugenephoto

There's several things I don't know here:

How good are you at reading emotional cues? Where are you going, what are you doing on these dates?

For instance, is she afraid to say "no" when you ask her on another date? Is she delaying or postponing dates? There are lots of clues that you probably have gathered by this moment.

But, I will tell you this. There is no need to ask her if you are on the fifth date. By the fifth date, you two know enough about each other. At the end of the date, simply move in for the kiss. You will know very quickly where you stand, or sleep, that night.

How do I improve my social game? Meeting new people, potential love interests, etc.
@randyaaron

Instead of constantly boring people with my own story I'm going to steal from my wife Claudia's story. In February 2009 she was out of a job, was going to lose her house, run out of money and then... what? Maybe move back to Argentina for the first time in 15 years?

No. She decided to up her social game. Meet more people. She signed up tango classes, painting classes, I wish she had taken a goddamned cooking class, she went to Spanish-speaking meet-ups, she signed up for dating services, she went to yoga classes every day, she asked all her friends who should she be meeting and got good advice (advice that ultimately led her to me!).

She was honest about what she wanted. She cut losses quickly. She wouldn't waste time on dinners (our first date was a "tea" date and nothing more). She kept disciplined and didn't chase after intrigue and false hopes. But she kept expanding her "list of things to do" so that her social network would expand.

Again, as the network gets bigger (in whatever you do: social life, business life, journalist life, etc.) the value goes up exponentially. And it worked for her. Now we're married! So:

- Picture the people you want to be around, and then make sure every day you get closer and closer to where they are.

- Be honest about what you want and who you are. While, of course, always being polite, don't sacrifice your soul for meaningless and fleeting rewards.

How do I end relationships (personal, business, etc.)? @chucklecoq

I can only answer by counter example. I have never ended a relationship of any sort well.

The last business relationship I ended I basically had a job as a partner at a private equity firm. I decided for no specific reason other than a general discomfort that I didn't want to be there. So I just walked out mid-meeting. Left all my stuff there. Never returned calls or emails and never went back to the office. They might still have my name on the website. I don't even know.

Very bad!

Same thing with relationships. My basic technique: Move to a new city. Very bad.

I wish I could follow my advice on this one. And I hope to do so in the future. So take it for what it's worth (i.e. I haven't been able to follow my own advice).

HONESTY. Be up front that you are unhappy and want to leave and it's not really open for discussion.

LOVE. Be sincere that you wish the best for the person. Even if you feel betrayed or angry in some way. Betrayal and anger will become part of ancient history after a short while.

If you don't end things in those two ways I know from very personal experience that there are only horrible, horrible consequences. We only have a short time on this planet. Goal #2 is to avoid horrible consequences to any of your actions.

What is the best way to meet new people? I'm quite introverted/shy but I do have a (very) tiny circle of (close) friends.
@binarymac

Good! You solved the first problem: having a tiny circle of close friends. Now, do one of the following:

ORGANIZE A DINNER CLUB. Everyone in your circle cooks for the others (do this one day every week or so). You rotate through the circle. The one challenge: everyone has to invite others to the dinner that nobody else knows.

ANOTHER TECHNIQUE: GUY OR GIRL: TAKE DANCE LESSONS. Preferably tango classes. Your bodies close, you rotate through the other people in the class, you talk before and after, and over time you plan tango outings, etc. This works. Ditto for cooking.

WHAT ARE YOUR INTERESTS? When I first moved to New York City I had one interest: chess. So I went to Washington Square Park and played everyone who sat around there playing all day. Next thing I knew, I was living with them (although not in the homeless shelter where half of them lived at).

12 STEP PROGRAMS: There's a 12 step program for everyone. Here's my experience with them.[1] You have a room full of people who have hit bottom in one way or the other and need to commune with others to get over it. Many of them have short skirts, pretty faces, and dramatic problems. What better way to meet people?

DRINKING

Why did you quit drinking?
@robin_ahn

Alcohol was great for reducing inhibitions so I could be more comfortable, for instance, on a date. There's no question that is a positive on alcohol. But then, as I continued drinking within my dating process I realized that bad things were happening. Very bad things. Here are some of the negatives:

SICK. I was getting sick more often. Including the flu.

I WAS GETTING LESS SLEEP. Probably for two reasons: Drinking alcohol happens at night so that's one strike against sleep. Also, alcohol has lots of sugar so I'd fall asleep and then pop awake at

1 http://bit.ly/fWS54A

3 in the morning and wouldn't be able to get back to sleep. Even one glass of wine does that to me.

I WAS GAINING WEIGHT. For my entire life I was my college weight. And suddenly... I was 15 pounds more! This was after a three month period of drinking every night. I had a gut! So I had to stop.

I WAS BECOMING A LOVE ADDICT. I wouldn't always understand the emotional cues of the people around me, a skill I always thought I was good at. I think alcohol was making me put attributes on people that they didn't have but that I wanted them to have. One addiction leads to another. And "love" is a painful addiction to have.

So I stopped. And that cleared the way for many good things to happen in my life.

These days I find that I can simulate the effect of alcohol by slightly slurring my words when I need those reduced inhibitions. That hypnotizes my body into thinking it is drinking. I mention this in "11 Unusual Ways to Be a Better Public Speaker."[1]

LOVE

Is love, marriage, children, and all of that just a waste of time and money in the end?
@jaisondm

I did not want to have children. (See, "Is it Bad I wanted my First Kid to be Aborted?"[2]) I was terrified about it. I thought marriage, children, and love would reduce my time for other pursuits and reduce my chances of success and happiness.

1 http://bit.ly/jFlvrL
2 http://bit.ly/g4a3os

And I was right. Sort of. I did get divorced. And raising children is very hard. I'm not really that great at it although I try.[1]

But, that said, I don't think the answer is renunciation of these things. Quite the opposite. The renunciates have it easy. They choose not to go through the pain so that life and salvation can be easier for them.

But there are no greater gurus than your children. There is no greater teacher of emotions then learning to live with someone. There is no greater poet to soothe your passions than the person you fall in love with. I wouldn't trade any of my bad experiences in these areas for anything. Probably love and children have cost me my money and my life many times over. But I'm still alive. And better for it.

What are the statistics of men cheating more than once? @LynnHasselbrgr

I don't know the exact statistics but my gut tells me if a man cheats once, he's going to cheat twice. I once read a story about a person who would fire anyone who cheated on his wife *"because if he can cheat on his wife, he can cheat me."* People cheat for many reasons: that they might not be happy in their marriage is only one of them. In which case, they should end their marriage.

However, a big reason men cheat is that they are addicts. They love the chase, they're insecure and need that chase, and then acceptance of the invitation to sex, to feel alive again. This might be a reaction not to the marriage but to any number of things that have happened since childhood.

So how do you treat an addiction? Can a person actually change? One possible solution is to go to a 12-step plan like *Sex and Love Addicts Anonymous* (SLAA).

I know many people who have successfully been able to go to SLAA and get over their love or sex addictions. But you have to

1 http://bit.ly/oLhh1v

treat it like you would treat any other illness. You cannot just say, *"no more cheating,"* because that will do nothing to solve the underlying causes of what happened.

One other statistic that I heard that may or may not be true: if a man cheats and then moves in with his new girlfriend there is a 95% chance it will not work out. Again, who knows? Nevertheless sometimes statistics are useful ledges to hang onto.

What do you do when someone you love is very depressed/ or sad?
@Unpacktherat

Most important: know that you cannot solve their problems. When people are depressed they are like an onion. The topmost skin is the OFFICIAL REASON they are depressed. Maybe someone didn't return a call or someone at work said something about then. However, if all you do is respond to (eat) that skin, it won't taste very good and it won't help anyone.

One layer down might be they are feeling shame over what that person said about them, or feelings of insecurity on why this person didn't call them back. The nameless person who is supposed to call back might not even know he or she has been placed on such an aggressive timeline. But the insecurity in your friend is there and is real. That is the next layer.

One further layer down, as we continue peeling this beautiful onion (since onions and garlic basically add positively to almost any food you can imagine except for maybe vanilla milkshakes), might be events that happened thirty years ago that began to trigger these insecurities.

And even a further layer down, the insecurities and shame might be triggered by events that happened 100 years ago to ancestors of your friend.

How are you going to solve these problems? How is your friend even going to do so? It is too difficult!

Neither of you can solve them. Therapists think they can by TALKING ABOUT THE PARENTS, perhaps, but the problems might even go deeper. The things making your friend sad are insurmountable if you try to tackle them directly.

What you can do is listen. That is all you do. Let your friend talk. Then she knows she has someone who will listen to her. That makes her happy. Makes her feel loved. Listen to and love your friend.

This way you can't solve the problems but you can redirect.

Did she exercise today? That always releases hormones that counteract sadness. Is she sleeping okay? Is she eating okay? If she is feeling bloated and weighed down to the Earth she will be sadder than if she is feels like she is flowing properly.

Then, I would slightly redirect in the direction of the *Daily Practice*[1] is she emotionally, mentally, and spiritually taking care of herself?

For each person that means different things. However, unless you have all four legs of that chair, all those areas of life in place, the chair will break and you will fall to the floor.

For example, is she feeling creative? (mental), is she practicing a sense of surrender and gratitude? (spiritual) and just by her being around you she is practicing the emotional muscle (since you are listening and being kind to her – so she clearly made the right choice in contacting you).

When the chair is built solidly on the four legs of the daily practice, and there is a nice cushion on it, she can sit again, and her mind and body will be able to relax. Thanks to you, and thanks to her, of course. The point is, this is perhaps the only way in which you can help, the real answers, the deep aha! Moments will only come from within her, all you can do is provide the space and support environment.

1 http://bit.ly/fuiRS9–

Love or career?
@Karlavigilante

They are the same. If they aren't the same, then figure out how to move towards a point where they are the same. There are no excuses in this.

Where should I go on my honeymoon?
@VeryStonemanEsq

Here's the problem with a honeymoon (in general): 3 hours in an airport, 3-10 hours flying someplace, 2 hours getting from airport to hotel, checking in, then resting after all of that, then eating too much food, getting sunburned, doing too many planned activities (instead of the most important activity that happens on a honeymoon), and then rushing back to airport and repeating process.

What a drag! Does twenty hours of traveling sound like fun to you? And spending another $10,000 in the process? And then maybe getting a tour of a lizard garden or whatever else you do on an average honeymoon?

People go to get away from the worries of life, the pressures of family and friends, to have privacy, to consummate, etc. So just do all of that, but without the hassles of all of the above.

Do the staycation, where you stay at home, but plan to do things you would never ever do at home. Don't make any plans with friends or family. Don't even tell them what you are doing. Send exotic postcards to them.

Then really make an effort to find new things in the area you think you know well. Worst case, go 20 minutes out and stay at a bed and breakfast or two.

Final result: More time with your new spouse. Less money spent. Less travel hassles. More energy. Probably better food (did you really think Club Med food was going to be better than the cheapest diner?). And probably more fun.

And, if you hate everything I said and disagree with me totally, you could try one of these things:

- Amangani[1] – Super vacation resorts around the world.
- Bible History Daily[2] – Why not go on a biblical archaeological dig?
- Samahita Retreat[3] – Yoga Spa

My best vacations happened when I had just started working a corporate job and I would take off a week just to explore the city I lived in. My worst vacations ever were probably my two honeymoons.

SEX

What's the easiest way to get into a threesome? @bear23

Not having been in one, I assume the easiest way (now that I think about it) is to use Craigslist and just put an ad up. It shouldn't be too hard.

That said, if you're a guy and want to meet women in bulk, who want to meet men, and who have the full spectrum of tastes and desires, then, go where they are.

If you hang out at the local chess club you're not going to meet women.

1 http://bit.ly/yhCwN
2 http://bit.ly/wotgiN
3 http://bit.ly/TGYhv

If you hang out at cooking class you are going to meet women who want to get married.

But if you go to yoga class and tango class then you're going to meet beautiful, sexy, women who are physically healthy, stretch the boundaries of what they are willing to attempt physically, and perhaps most importantly, they want to meet men. Not everyone, of course (if that were the case then there would be more men in these classes than women) but some definitely. So stop watching football on a Sunday afternoon (i.e. no women) and go to the nearest tango class (lots of women).

For me, I like one on one and falling in love. My guy friends always think I'm like a girl. The second I have sex with a girl I fall in love, which means I then get in trouble. I can't imagine getting in trouble with two girls. And on top it, performance anxiety with one girl is enough, I don't need the headaches of two.

How can I have charisma?
@PriscillaPWood

It feels like I have ego if I answer this question. I can't claim to be charismatic. But I do know what people will respond to in the long run. Try to work very hard at this list:

- BE YOURSELF. Meaning: don't be afraid to say what you mean. Don't hurt anyone by doing it but don't be afraid to speak up and stand up for what you think is the right thing. Don't be a follower.

- BE HONEST. I've written before about the power of honesty. What happens when you always speak the truth is that eventually, with practice, your words speak truth to the universe. Your words become law. What you say has power.

  People respond to THE FORCE of your words because they know each word has impact. Think about it, there are so many ways in which we lie, in tiny ways, even to ourselves. But if you stop it, or work on it, or practice being honest, the benefits are beyond what can be imagined.

- BE KIND: always have good will towards people. I really believe in what Buddha said to his son Rahula (Which I describe in "Was Buddha a Bad Father"[1]): *"Before, during, and after any thought, speech, or action FOCUS on whether or not you are doing harm."*

When you just do these things, this is going to sound corny, an inner light will shine through. People will see it. That is real charisma. I hope one day I can have it.

In marriage how often should a man/woman "get paid" or have sex with their significant other?
@Psfs

First off, you use an interesting phrase: *"get paid."* Given the scarcity of characters we have on Twitter (140), you could have just said, how often should one have sex with their spouse? Instead, you had to explain it.

So "get paid" sort of implies one side owes something to the other side (the man or the woman, you are careful enough to point out).

I would say it is better if you both want it. How can that happen? Well, keeping the paid analogy, why don't you do a little of your wife's job and she does a little of yours? Try that every day. See if it increases the feeling of partnership or the feeling of wanting the other in your life. Then try this: have sex every day for a year.

That seems like a lot of work. Particularly if you are older. How can you have an orgasm every day? Well, who says you have to have that? But have sex every day for a year anyway, no pressures, just fun.

---

1 http://www.jamesaltucher.com/2011/01/was-buddha-a-bad-father/

Check out this article[1] on a couple that had sex every day for a year. It sounds pretty good. I think I'll try it.

Good friend is cheating on wife. Should I tell the wife? – Asked anonymously through DM

NO! Don't be in the middle. There are many reasons why someone cheats. There are many issues that the person is working out individually and also as a couple. Why make the personal problems of a couple the personal problems of a "triple" (when you include yourself).

I have seen this several times. Where a friend is cheating. Even when I've seen people close to me being cheated on, for instance, I see the husband of a good friend out with another woman. I'm friends with the wife but not the husband so could have easily told the wife but I chose to stay out of it.

Why did I stay out of it? Because sooner or later the wife finds out. And all shit hits the fan. Why be in the middle of shit spraying on your face? The couple will work it out sooner or later. One way or the other. For better or for worse. In sickness and in health.

How do I go through life loving just one woman when I see floods of beautiful women every day? Shouldn't monogamy be dissolved? @eefeanyi

Let's look at the upside and downside of this. Obviously there's one downside to being monogamous: you can't have sex with other women/men. Sex with someone new is a great, exciting thing. Even if it comes bottled up with intrigue, chasing, and an eventual end.

So what are the upsides of monogamy?

- You definitely get to know someone a lot better.

---

1 http://nyti.ms/wHIbx4

- With that knowledge, you penetrate not only the body but many different layers you didn't know existed before, particularly if you are serious about continuing to fall in love with the person you are with.
- If you jump from person to person (literally) you never get to experience that depth. But, as I mentioned in the "Diseases that Billionaires Get,"[1] it's hard (like anything that's worth it) to stick with monogamy. Perhaps the most important thing (for men) to know, is that scientific evidence suggests that monogamous relationships lead to a greater life expectancy.

MARRIAGE

What is the purpose of marriage?
@RobertSinn

Marriage is a gift you give to your spouse. It's a gift that says, *"I have fully enjoyed our past together, I fully enjoy our present together, and now I want to devote the rest of my future to helping you achieve your goals, to being with you, to you being with me, and to taking care of you (or vice versa) when we are old and sick, as we almost assuredly will be."*

You cannot give a gift like that lightly. The pieces have to be set up in the right spots. Everything has to be aligned. The slightest piece off could mean that your position has gone from "strikingly interesting" to "dubious." The seeds of disaster are always right there in front of you if they exist.

One area where Claudia and I differ, for instance, is that she likes to travel. I don't. But I've succumbed. We have been all over the world since we met, which fortunately has been much to my enjoyment. One way she's "sacrificed" if you call it that, is that I

1 http://bit.ly/qMghRZ

have two kids. Two kids are a lot of work! But she loves them and it works.

But the rest of the position on the board works. So I was happy to give her this gift and I hope she was happy to give this gift to me.

But do you have to be legally married? @RobertSinn

Of course, the answer is *"No."* You don't have to be anything. But there's something psychological about being physically married. You go from *"what am I going to do with Claudia tomorrow"* or *"this week"* or *"this month"* to *"Where should Claudia and I live fifteen years from now?"* And how do we get there together, hand in hand. If you can get that feeling without being legally married then power to you. But for me, I can't.

The past and the future co-mingle once that marriage certificate is issued. If marriage is a gift then getting legally married puts the wrapping on that gift. It makes the gift pretty.

So that answers: *What is the purpose of marriage,* but let's do a quick checklist on The *Should You Get Married Checklist*:

ETHICS. You should both have similar ethical standards. Standards about non-violence, telling the truth, feelings about adultery. Feelings about what you want in life (does this have to do with ethics? Of course, because if you want similar things then you will feel similar feelings of envy or non-envy as the occasion arises).

In New York City, I go to Grand Central a lot to take the train home. Whenever I see a man and a woman kissing right by the train-gates I think one thing: adultery. I would say about 1/3 of New York City marriages are adulterous. That is their business. But why are people taking trains to two different places in the suburbs? It's because they live with two different spouses. Again, it's their business. But doesn't seem for me like the most relaxing and pleasurable way to live life.

DISCIPLINE. Do you both work in similar fashion towards your goals? Do you both keep clean? Equal standards of cleanliness are very important. Claudia is very clean, for instance, and I'm disgusting. But I work towards being similar to her. It's important to me. If it wasn't, then attraction would subside faster than it normally does in any long-term relationship.

There is a saying: put a dime in a glass jar every time you have sex with your girlfriend/wife the first year. After that, take a dime out every time you have sex. You'll never empty the jar.

Your goal, if all of these boxes are checked, is to empty that jar as quickly as possible. Equal standards of cleanliness and discipline are part of that after that blissful first year.

Do you both eventually want to move towards a life of material pursuit to one less ambitious, more in tune with contentment? This goes along with religion. If one is into New Age Born Again Christian Astrology and the other is an atheist then these are 100% different belief systems. So this suggests you might have great chemistry but in the long run, even five years out, you might have great problems. (Nothing wrong with New Age Born Again Christian Astrology and nothing wrong with atheism. But they are different).

The notion of contentment is very important. If one side wants to make $100 million and be a high-powered banker in the city and the other person wants to eventually live in a small house by the ocean then, again, the first year might have been huge chemistry but in the long run you're going to drift to people who have similar feelings about long-term contentment.

Physically. You should always have similar ideas about what constitutes good health and the methods for keeping the good health. If one of you works out every day and the other never does then attraction would be lost fast. Also, the one who works out every day will have consistently higher libido. And the one who doesn't work out every day will feel badly about how they look and will end up with lower libido. If libidos are way out of whack then, that's it, the marriage is in trouble and adultery is around the corner.

"Physical" also means how much energy you have. If one is filled with energy from eating well, sleeping well, exercising, etc. then the other person needs to keep up. Again, this can all be covered up the first year or two. But in marriage, things like this are seeds that turn into a big tree. And you can be at the bottom of that tree while your partner has climbed the top and is staring out at the mountains on the other side of the river.

Mentally. This doesn't mean you have to be equally smart, or like the same books and movies. In every Woody Allen movie they all seem to like the same boring operas and then break up at the end. But I do think it means having a similar curiosity, a similar love of having things you are passionate about, a similar eagerness to explore the unknown (and by the way, I'm not saying you should both want to explore the unknown but have a similar predilection one way or the other towards exploring the unknown).

Emotionally. There's the notion called "splitting the difference" – one side is always aggressive, the other side is always passive. One side always wants to clean the house, the other side always wants to mess up the house. And this difference gets wider after marriage. So there has to be a constant recognition, *"Okay, this is where I'm splitting the difference"* and try to bring that difference back to even. A conscious decision on both sides. It's a daily check because it happens every day. You have to consciously think: *"this is what she would do,"* so you do it first. There's a piece of dog shit on the floor. I should pick it up first (By the way, I could probably never marry someone with a dog). There's a light on in the other room. I don't care but I should shut it down first. And she should be thinking the same way. He probably wants that Amazon Kindle Case so he doesn't break his Kindle. I'll get it.

WILLINGNESS TO SURPRISE. The senses get dulled over time. If someone keeps scratching an itch, it eventually has no effect, or you end up with a bloody scab. You need different ways to approach surprise. To bring you back to that feeling you had the first moment you kissed.

One guy once wrote me last Valentine's Day and said, *"It's 5pm Valentine's Day, I have no idea what to do?"* I never heard from him again after that but here was my answer:

Try one of these two things. With your handy waiter pad, fill it up with notes of love. Put it all over the house, so that even a year from now she might find a note in an obscure spot. Or make a blog, where every post is a different reason you love her. You can't ever forget the desire to surprise that you had that first week, month, year.

SPIRITUAL SIMILARITIES. Ultimately, we are all on a path. Not to see who makes the most money. Or who can bowl the most strikes in game. Or who can do the most pushups. But what are the attributes I need to pursue to find contentment in life. You're 30 years old, say, and thinking of getting married. 60 years is a long time if you think you are going to be in a monogamous relationship that long. It's good to check the box that you are on a similar path towards contentment.

By the way, the above checklist is not just to decide if you should get married to X, but if you, personally, should get married at all! You might not be ready to be "ethical" in terms of adultery. You might not have any clue what sorts of long-term goals surrounding contentment you have. Who knows? I just think this is a good starting point.

What is the ONE piece of advice do you have if you have a newborn baby?
@euros

Nine months ago a lot of people had unprotected sex. How do I know this? Because I've been asked this exact question three times in the past week: I congratulate these people on having such pleasure in their lives nine months ago. It's a great thing to orgasm knowing that you might've have also created another human being to add to the seven billion that already exist.

I reminded the questioner that I was far from the expert.

- I wanted my first daughter to be aborted.
- I want my kids to be lesbians.
- I played poker the night my daughter was born.
- Some would argue my kids should be taken away from me because I don't want them to go to college.

So from beginning to end I might be a screw-up.

But I will give it an answer: because who better to answer the questions in the King's court than the Jester himself. The one who has been so foolish and who has nothing to lose (a jester's position, in every movie I've ever seen about medieval times, seems to be infinitely secure).

My one advice: take care of and nurture your relationship with your wife. Why?

Because for years your wife and you lived in your own private island. You made jokes to each other that nobody could understand. You spoke your own private language. You shared hopes, dreams, kisses only with each other.

Suddenly, the worst thing possible happens. A 1 foot tall human moves into your house. Just like that she moves in. Who the hell invited her? She doesn't speak English. She shits on the floor and you have to clean it. She cries a lot.

And it doesn't get better. In fact, for the first two years it gets worse. Wait till she starts walking. Now she's hurting herself by running into things. No normal human being would run into that TV set but she did. And then, ugh, she gets toilet trained. Now you have to make sure she makes it to the bathroom in time. Or there will be shit and urine everywhere and you have to get down on your hands and knees and clean it up. Did you ever think, when you were 15 years old and planning on being an astronaut, that you would be on your hands and knees cleaning up the shit of this uninvited guest.

And what limited space you and your wife have (you're just starting out in life: your free from your own parents, schools, maybe your first corporate jobs where you were no better than slaves) and now space is stolen from you. Your child needs a bedroom, then maybe a playroom, then maybe toys.

In fact, your child needs to be constantly entertained. It sucks! Taking care of a child is a Zen experience and I mean that in a negative way (almost all Zen "experiences" are negative). Just take the basic fact: you are sitting on the floor in the lotus position for an hour doing nothing. Boring and painful. The Lotus position is not designed to be a pleasurable position for the body. By the time you get up, your legs have fallen asleep, the blood rushes back in full force and the pain for at least sixty seconds is as if you had your legs amputated without anesthetic.

Taking care of a child is Zen because you can only focus on the child. You can't focus on anything else. For hours. And by the way, that's mostly your wife. Or your babysitter, who could care less about your kid for the most part.

Here's what I did by accident the first week after my kid was born:

On the way to playing poker my then-wife asked me to take the garbage out. Instead, I did the worst thing you could ever do.

There was a garbage bag sitting outside the bedroom. I took that garbage bag of brand new clothes instead of the garbage bag that was, of course, supposed to go in the garbage can.

It was all her clothes that she was going to wear for Easter. My first child was born at the end of February. Which means, with Easter around the corner we were still in that special window where a woman's body has not quite fully recovered, not quite achieved its former glamor (which is the hidden secret because your wife is allowed to acknowledge that and plan for it but you must never mention it). She had carefully planned, stitch by stitch, dresses, undergarments, socks, everything, what she would wear for Easter.

I threw out all her Easter clothes.

Then I went to play poker. I lost $500 that night. Walking home across the park "Madison Green" (now home of the famous "Shake Shack" hamburger joint) at 4 in the morning I had to jump and stomp as high as possible to clear out the rats which covered every possible inch of the path through the park. They scurried away and at that moment it occurred to me.

I was in big trouble. And I was. Several weeks later (since I hid the facts of what I had done and even pleaded ignorance until there was no way out) I had to get down on my knees and cry apologies and perhaps even threaten my own life or the life of my zero year old to somehow cancel out all the pain that was caused.

I say this not as one event that should be avoided but as a cascading series of events that occurs when child #1 is born. Events that when added up irrevocably change the binding that was once two and you have to adjust to the School House Rock / De La Soul song *"Three Is the Magic Number."* Yes it is, as the lyrics go, it's the magic number. No more twos.

For me, three never became magic. And neither did four. And ultimately my marriage was gone. And ultimately I got divorced and I met Claudia. I can argue for me it worked out for the best. Maybe for you it will work out for the best also. But kids want their parents to stay together. So this is a long of saying...

The most important advice I can give when your first child is born is pay attention to your wife. She will take care of you when you are sick. And many years later, she will think about you when you are long gone.

Best advice for newlyweds? ;)
@abbymaries

I'm perfectly qualified for this question, having been a newlywed now twice!

I think there's four parts of a relationship:

1. That initial honeymoon period where it's all goo-goo love and is very nice and what we always remember and/or fantasize about.

2. The "wedding planning" when everything involves taking the relationship to that all-important next level. We almost forget the past and the future when we are going through this. The planning is all-consuming.

3. The real honeymoon. The thing that happens there is we start thinking about the future. The long-term future. Right after you get married you realize, *"Wow, I'm going to probably spend forty to sixty years with this person."* And you start planning and imagining how that will happen.

4. Babies. But let's not worry about that yet. You're a newlywed.

So you're in part 3. Where you start thinking about the future. Where will you live? How will you afford it? When will you have kids? How will you afford their education and health? Should you rewrite your wills? Should you now start a business or settle in for the long-run at your corporation?

So much future to plan for! Sixty years! Holy shit!

But... you can't ever forget about that initial honeymoon period.

Where you wake up next to someone and feel surprised that he or she is actually THERE. You can touch them! They are there for you. There is something new every day you learn.

Remember: there's something new every day that you can learn from the other person. Some new passion you can incite. Some new smile you can create on the other person's face.

Planning for the future takes up a lot of mental energy. So don't ever forget about that initial passion and how happy it made you both feel. Try every day to surprise the other person with your memories of it and how happy you were then. You both were.

Finally, the honeymoon never lasts forever, but it's fun to see if you can be the first to make it last that long.

DIVORCE

When do you decide to leave someone? At what point is it really over? Even if you share children?
@brainybetty

This not a simple question. Particularly when there are children involved. You should always try to make things work. But, there are exceptions:

1. Is the person abusive to you in any way? This could be the result of a temperament they've had since their childhood. It also can be a result of your own temperament, which is allowing abuse without setting boundaries.

2. Is the person abusive to the kids in any way? Then the kids must be removed from the person immediately. When someone is abusive towards another it is already a pattern, and one that is hard to break. If this person has abused your child in

any way then there is simply no turning back. The person needs help, and your children need to be far from that sickness.

3. Most situations are not so direct. And abuse is subtle. So my thermometer is: have the arguments worn you down to the bone. Where you can't even look at the person without the two of you arguing? In my own situation I was arguing so much with my ex-wife the police had to be called and I had to spend the night at a motel. When things like that start to happen then there is nothing good that can be the result. It's time to move on.

One time my youngest came into the kitchen where her mom and I were arguing. She asked: "*Umm, Josie [her older sister] wants to know if you guys are going to stay together.*" Somehow Josie had convinced her younger sister to broach this question to us. They were scared. They were confused. Just like the stock market and the world economy, kids abhor uncertainty. After that I knew it was over.

Never forget that the kids want love. They don't want hate. Four happy parents (when you mix the step-parents) are much better than two very unhappy, constantly arguing parents.

If I make a billion shall I rub it in the ex-wife's face? @TraderStrong

No! There's that expression *"the best revenge is living well."* It doesn't say, *"the best revenge is smothering your ex's face with your success."* In fact, I'm going to change the expression slightly. *"The best revenge is just being happy."* The statement is almost a logical impossibility. You can't be really happy if you are consumed with thoughts of revenge.

There are quite a few people I want revenge on. I know I won't be happy until those feelings of revenge start to go down and eventually disappear. How do I do that?

Every time I think, *"man, I'm going to get that guy back"* or whatever, I catch myself and think *"not useful."* I won't be happy until I stop thinking "not useful" thoughts. It's hard to catch yourself in the middle of one of these thoughts. You have to practice. Practice is the water; the feelings of revenge are like a rock in your head.

Eventually water withers away the rock. When no rocks are left, you have a clean sandy beach, then the ocean, then the horizon. Happy.

LIFE

I spend a great deal of time holding myself back. How do I stop it??
@wiztrader

The structure of your question is revealing because of the two question marks. As if your own body ("holding myself back") is totally out of your control. The use of the word "it," again implying your inability to move forward is somehow an "it," outside of you, controlling you. So let's ask: What is controlling you?

I will tell you. Your parents are. Your friends are. Your spouse is. Your job is. Your colleagues are. Your children are. So many people have expectations of you. Each one draws a circle around you. You can't move beyond each person's circle without disappointing their expectations.

And so where can you stand? You stand in the center, in the tiniest circle of all, the tiny circle that is the intersection of all the many circles drawn around you.

You need to step out of the circles. Forget about "it" for a second. There is no "it." There is you. You need to step out of those circles but it's not so easy. You've just spent the first half of your life keeping inside of them.

To step out in one second is impossible or , at the very least, hard. You are now a spy. A spy on your own life. There are enemies everywhere, keeping track of your position. You must attempt to fool them.

Do something a little different. Finger-paint. Take the wrong subway. Go vegetarian for a week. Leave in the middle of the day and don't comeback. Go to a museum instead. Write a one page novel. Give advice to someone who didn't ask for it and doesn't want it.

My favorite: return an email from 2007. Start it: *"Sorry for the small delay."* Write an email to someone you hate and say, *"How's it going today?"*

You can't jump forward tillyou learn how to step forward. To step forward you have to start breaking through these tight circles wrapped around you. You have to practice what it's like to move outside the circles.

In the movie THX-1138 (George Lucas, pre Star Wars), all of the inhabitants of the underworld are told the world above has been destroyed by radiation. So they have to live in this tightly controlled 1984ish world with tight controls. The main characters, as they do, fall in love. They are chased for breaking the rules. Eventually they hit above ground and realize it is not wracked with radiation. It is, in fact, a paradise.

Give yourself time. Practice stepping outside the circles. Eventually you will break free into the above world. And nothing will ever hold you back again.

How do you take that next step towards living and adventure when life is full of inertia to stay silent and still? @kaisdavis

On any given day the general tendency is to just do your normal routine. The "normal routine" is a jealous beast. It doesn't want us to do anything new. So it basically has us in the routines that keep us trapped into continuing its follies: We eat heavy, greasy food, which weighs us down and keeps us sluggish. We drink – which further removes the methods by which we can escape out of the box we've carved out for ourselves. We go to our shit jobs so we can pay back our student loan debts. We hang out with our friends. I would like to hang out more with friends. But it's hard to do that and plan for the exciting future which we can rightfully claim to be ours.

We live our normal routines because we have been told forever that's how we become happy. We become afraid to break out of the routine. To risk the unhappiness that might occur.

The key ultimately is to, first, figure out how to get rid of the inertia and then the real living will come.

I have had periods of real inertia. Where all I could do was sit around and be depressed. The only way I've been able to get out of it is to make sure every day I'm checking the box on the following items:

- am I improving physically?

- am I improving emotionally – getting rid of negative influences, surrounding myself with positive influences?

- am I improving mentally – writing down lists of ideas every day?

- am I improving spiritually – being grateful for what I have, focusing on the present moment, surrendering to whatever higher power or subconscious power, that I might believe in?

How can one be both smart and good looking?
@Mike_Ocsbig

It's hard to be smart and good-looking. So I told god before I was born I would only take the former. Just to guarantee it.

What defines you as a person?
@Morgan_03

My goal is to have nothing define me as a person.

Really? Not even "loving father, caring husband, successful entrepreneur?
@Morgan_03

All of these things are good things. I want to, of course, be a caring father, and I want to achieve success in a variety of silos in my life. But when I'm on my deathbed I ultimately want to be just me.

I want nothing to define me. Nothing I can look back on and say "that was me" because all of that is artificial and man-made. Any definition at all is limiting. At the end of my life, when I'm staring into god knows what, I want to be limitless.

What would James Altucher do if he was 25 years old right now?
@rballe33

Not everyone could be a Mark Zuckerberg and start a new business from scratch and watch it grow into billions. So the obvious answer of "start a business" doesn't really apply. Starting a business is hard, needs money, and requires you to know what people are missing in their lives. Also, a consumer-oriented business is the hardest sort of business to start, but if you have no enterprise experience, then it's also difficult to start a business selling to the enterprise.

Believe it or not, here's what I would recommend: work at a big company, learn everything about them, find out what they are missing, and after two years start a business supplying the things you find that they were missing.

This, in fact is what I did (I was 26 and not 25) when I went to work for HBO. If you are vigilant, you will find many things they are missing and even if they don't become your first client, if you build your network while you are on the job, you will find first clients for your service. (Be service-oriented, then transform to product-oriented. This way you are profitable right away).

What's your perfect day like? @brainybetty

I'm not going to answer on what my perfect day is. But what your perfect day could look like. Try to check these boxes:

- ☐ Be around people who love you

- ☐ Come up with ten new ideas for businesses you can start, how you can improve your job, books or articles you can write, gifts or favors you can give people you love, ideas for how you can help others, etc. Just come up with ten new ideas.

- ☐ Kiss someone. Preferably a lot. Kids are good. Or a spouse.

- ☐ Do something creative. Ideally something creative that either makes you money or there's way to connect the dots between creativity and money. Creativity doesn't always have to equal "more money" but it helps. Even if its a business idea. Businesses are creative. Not just paintings or novels.

- ☐ I sleep eight or nine hours. Or, heck, ten hours.

- ☐ I find a time in the middle of the day to be by myself for a bit.

- ☐ Part of that time I can use to read a book.

Life

- ☐ Part of it I can use to just be quiet and not think or worry about anything.
- ☐ I take a huge BM. Nothing is better than that.
- ☐ I avoid all junk food and eat no more than two healthy meals a day. Some people say you should eat lots of little meals all day long. Maybe they are right. But I find that its hard to eat "little" meals and that I tend to eat lots of big meals all day long whenever I try that approach.
- ☐ I have feelings of gratitude towards everyone I meet. This is hard and is a practice (for me).
- ☐ Ideally I meet or talk to new people during the day but I don't do more than one meeting in the morning and one meeting in the afternoon.
- ☐ I exercise. Ideally yoga with Claudia.
- ☐ I read a spiritual text of some sort.
- ☐ I read good fiction.

Believe it or not, I find on most days I can do most of the above. Tell me in the comments how your ideal day might be different or what you think I should add to mine.

CRAPPY PEOPLE

What do you do when you can't ignore the crappy person because you have to report to them?
@shoaglun

Here's the issue with crappy people – they are the people that drive you crazy the most, the ones you can't stop thinking about and the ones you are constantly imagining arguments, responses, counter-responses, things they did that were wrong, etc.

I sometimes wake up thinking about these things and it is a discipline (hard) to divert myself because almost by definition they are the people you can't avoid. Bosses, colleagues, family, friends of friends, etc. That is why they are in our lives in the first place, else you would ignore them and move on.

The trick is to just not engage. If they want to provoke, or yell, or spit, or do something crappy, then:

- Be as polite as possible but don't' respond to anything provoking. Silence and minimal words are best things to do.

- Remove yourself from the situation/phone/location as quickly as possible.

Why be around someone crappy when you can be around someone you love?

An interesting thing happens. A few months ago I heard a phrase "the herx reaction." It occurs when you start taking antibiotics. Sometimes you get worse first.

When you don't engage, the crappy people go crazy. You know the phrase, "ignoring is the best revenge." When you ignore or don't engage with whoever is trying to provoke you, you cut off their supply of food and oxygen. They feed off of being crappy to you. Don't feed the monster!

It's up to you to stop feeding them. And at first they will scream in anger and hunger. They desperately want to be fed!

Then, bit by bit they will starve. Then finally, they will be extinguished. You will have trained them in that you do not respond to crappiness. And you will be more alive than ever.

What is the best way to deal with a co-worker who consistently discredits you in a passive aggressive way? @robertsgm

Four things:

1. Never argue with him.

2. Never gossip about him behind his back.

3. Never blame him.

4. Never respond to anything he says other than direct, factual information or a simple "yes" or "no."

In other words: No Dancing. This person is an inconsequential bug. Don't think about him, talk about him, talk to him, or "think to him" in any way. This creates the atmosphere/ecosystem/training where it will his passive aggressiveness will ultimately have no effect on you.

Remember, he was probably beaten as a child, or rejected by girls, or harassed by other bosses or co-workers and now he is trying to do all of that to you. Don't let any of it stick on your mind, your emotions, or your body. It's hard. But you will do it. And that's how he will be trained like a dog, that he is to treat you better.

And once he starts treating you better, give him credit when credit is deserved. Eventually this person will want to be your best friend. But by then you will have long moved on.

What should you do if you're avoiding a friend and you don't know why?
@estheria

This has happened to me repeatedly. You have to ask yourself one thing: Am I avoiding him today simply because I avoided him yesterday. An "avoidance bubble" of sorts. In other words, are you feeling so much shame about avoiding your friend that that it's preventing you from reaching out today. If the answer is "no" then move onto the next paragraph.

Something is wrong. Your body and mind are telling you to stay away. You can do some self-enquiry and start listing reasons why your mind might be telling you to stay away, but your mind might not answer. Your body and mind might be keeping it a secret. But respect the secret. Don't force it. You are a busy person. If you're body is telling you, *"this person is bad for you right now. Stay away."* Then after briefly considering the reasons why this might be, take the advice: stay away.

I hate calling people back that are energy drainers. Do you think I will have bad karma if I don't call them back?
@Bert_Hancock

Unless it's the IRS, there's rarely a need to call back the people who drain you. I say this for the general case (if someone's in the hospital and it's their dying breath then you might as well pick up, for instance).

Let's think about it out loud for a second.

If you don't call them back several things happen:

You save energy instead of lose it during the 30 minutes that phone call would've taken. What will you do with those thirty minutes? Maybe you'll walk by the river? Maybe you'll take out a notebook and be creative. Maybe you'll call your kids and tell them you love them?

Almost everything you can do that's positive will be better than talking to a zombie that wants to drain you.

The person whose call you didn't return will begin to hate you and will stop calling you. Great! Youve trained them well. Future energy will be preserved.

Energy is finite for everything in the universe. We run out of it. Eventually the big bang will reverse and implode. So whatever you can do to build energy (see below question) and preserve it (see this question) is critical for the quality of your life.

But there's one more question that needs to be asked: why does someone drain you? Sometimes we let people drain us?

We feed off of it. We get provoked. We attack back. We engage in the "game," the "dance," we get in the three-legged race with the people we hate most. Part of avoiding energy draining is not only training the other person but really being honest with yourself.

Why does this person have permission to call you in the first place? So the first steps come not whether or not to return a call but to prevent the call from even happening. And this requires constant awareness of who you are associating yourself with.

You ultimately become like the people you associate with. Start today being more aware of who those people are.

What do you do when someone won't forgive? And when they have no desire for owning their part, only hating & feeling like victim?
@asplenia

We all deal with these people every day. These are called "crappy people" in my overly simplistic terminology. And guess what?

Crappy people aren't the neighbors down the street. Or the people from the distant past you never see anymore. Crappy people, by definition, are the people often closest to you: family, friends, colleagues, and bosses.

The question is: why do you care so much what is going on inside of these other people. Only worry what's going on inside you. And if someone is inside of your head, then get them out. So the only answer really is to ignore them. If you can't ignore them completely, then don't engage with them. Say "hi" and don't let them press buttons. Respond politely. Be pleasant. But get away as soon as possible so you can come back on the computer and read my blog.

Would the world be a better place if each person in the world had a no retaliation allowed, one free punch per year?
@icekevin

Haha, I know what you mean. What you are really asking is: if everyone was slightly afraid that they would be a recipient of that no-retaliation one punch per year then perhaps people might behave better to each other.

The other day I was in Grand Central Gourmet. At rush hour when everyone is trying to buy some last minute food before catching their trains, I accidentally bumped into an older woman (in her 70s or 80s). Just brushed against her. She shoved me so hard I fell to the floor and dropped my own bag of food.

Should I have punched her? Would that have made the world a better place? Maybe she was a survivor of concentration camps? Maybe her father beat her so now she felt comfortable the rest of her life beating others. Maybe her son or daughter had died an early death. I have no idea what was going on in her life really.

Why then, punch her? Even if I could. Would that make the world a better place if that was my once a year no-retaliation punch?

No.

Instead she became my greatest teacher that day. A day where I had already met many fascinating other teachers. I had to quickly pick myself up, pick my food up, get on my train, and not let my mind be crowded with thoughts of anger for her.

That's pretty hard! I dare you to try it. That's much harder than punching her. I couldn't stop wondering, *"why did she shove me so violently? Who would do that?"* Heck, I'm still thinking of it.

But eventually the thoughts did simmer down. And on the train ride back I was able to enjoy a book. And I was happy when I got home and was able to see the Hudson River from my house, and the leaves on the trees turning all sorts of colors. I was able to log onto my computer and answer emails. I was able to come up with ideas. I was able to enjoy dinner. I was able to write a post.

I was able to save the world. No punching.

MOTIVATION

I know that you write a lot about getting motivated when times are bad, but how do you stay motivated when times are good?
@derekwhurst

Every day wake up and pretend you are a superhero. You're Clark Kent. Nobody knows you are a superhero. But you wake up and you get out of your bed and you have a mission: you have to save at least one life today.

Repeat it to yourself: I have to save a life today. Who will it be?

Then the rest of the day, be on the lookout for how you can help save that live. Or, if you must, go ahead and save the world.

It's a costume game. It's make-believe. And it works.

What motivated you to when you were 20, 30, 40 years old? @marty7higgins

When I was 20 I wanted to write the "Great American Novel." Now, why in hell would a healthy young 20 year old with no experience in life want to sit in front of a computer for 4-5 hours a day for maybe one to two years with little or no hope of actually getting published? In fact, I probably spent five years in front of that computer for five to ten hours a day.

One reason: sex. I though, perhaps misguidedly, that if I was the author of a great novel then despite what I perceived to be my other disadvantages, that girls would want to have sex with me. Lots of girls. Any girl I wanted, in fact.

What was wrong with me? A lots of things. For starters I lacked self-confidence. If I had spent those five years trying to have more confidence in myself, trying to fill the emptiness I thought a finished novel would fill, then not only would I have been a lot happier during that time, I would've had a lot more time on my hands (instead of writing four unpublished novels) and I probably would've been having sex with many more women.

By 30 I had the same goal. But then, instead of the great American novel, I thought that having a million dollars or more would do the trick. By the way, writing novels does do the trick. You get a lot of confidence (temporarily, until you slip back to old habits), and confidence gets you all the sex you want. Not money but being able to stand up and assert: *"I can rule the world if I want to but I just don't feel like it right now."*

Now in my 40s finally, I have some confidence. So my goals are different. I have a healthy relationship with my wife. She's beautiful and she loves me. I think.

Now, I want freedom. Freedom from what? I don't know yet. But I know there's still some emptiness inside of me. I know that every day I try to fill it in various small ways. I look for a path when I know, intellectually, that a path is needed. One day I'll find the right path. And I know it will be inside me. But now I'm still looking for that elusive freedom from the forest which on occasion clouds my brain and soul.

How do I motivate others?
@AmanAlam

Basically, if your bodies are aligned, if you are keeping healthy physically, emotionally, mentally, and spiritually then you will shine and glow and be a beacon to others. That's the only way to truly motivate others.

Else the ones you are trying to motivate will sense where your bodies are weak and you will come across as false.

Which gives you more satisfaction, reinventing your own life or inspiring others to reinvent theirs? Why?
@iChmpneGrl

About a year ago I got sick of talking about stocks. Everyone wants stock tips. They think if they buy a stock and it goes up then they will be happier than they are now. That they will be more "safe." Some of my stock tips would go up , some would go down. When the stocks would go up, I would never hear from people again. When the stock would go down, everyone would send me angry notes.

So if along the way to happiness there's a lot of potential for anger, then it's not a true happiness. It's not even a true road.

I wanted to reinvent myself. And the way I reinvented myself is by writing a blog that shows how I reinvented myself and maybe that gives a little inspiration to help other people find the right way to reinvent their own selves.

People are still angry at me. But it's for their own reasons that have nothing to do with me. And I'm happier.

SUCCESS

How do you define success?
@TalentedBlonde

A friend of mine had breakfast with a well-known billionaire. All the billionaire kept doing for the entire breakfast was complain about how Larry Page has $18 billion and he *"only has $2 billion."*

Most people set goals and when they achieve those goals they think two things: *"Wow, I'm successful!"* and then... *"Wait a second. I want more!"*

We have been, as a society, brainwashed into thinking that the trappings of success (money, fame, promotions at a job) will get us to happiness. We've been conditioned and then enslaved by the slave masters of flesh, bank accounts, vanity, and the futility of thinking we can change things, we can find a path that will fill the emptiness inside.

Success ultimately boils down to the questions we ask ourselves which are related to *The Daily Practice,*[1] which I recommend:

1. Are we PHYSICALLY healthy?

2. Are we EMOTIONALLY healthy? Do we surround ourselves with people we love and who love us and avoid "the dance" with the people who bring us down?

3. Are we MENTALLY healthy? i.e. do we generate good ideas and use those ideas to benefit ourselves and others?

---

1 http://bit.ly/fuiRS9

4. Are we SPIRITUALLY healthy? i.e. do we have a good sense of "surrender" and use that sense to walk through life with humility, gratitude and reverence.

External success allows us the freedom to pursue these internal successes. That's real success! And we never achieve it but always, continuously strive for it. Success is a practice.

In your opinion/experience, what defines success? @texandcoda

When I first made a lot of money I thought: *"This is it! I succeeded in New York. I'm on top of the world."*

Less than three years later I was dead broke and lost my house. I was worse than dead broke. I was probably over a million in debt. And I had no friends. I lost them all.

Then I did it again. And again, and again. And each time I let it give birth to an uglier and uglier failure.

So I had to redefine it for myself. What does success mean to me now? Simply an ability to pursue the Daily Practice I outline. I don't want houses, or boats, or big vacations. I want FREEDOM.[1] Freedom to pursue my passions, to spend time with my daughters and wife, to get in shape, to stay emotionally healthy (which means 100% surrounding myself with uplifting people), to be mentally healthy (the ability and time to write), and spiritually healthy (the ability to read and have time and reduce my desire for all the toys that success in America usually implies).

I want to die when I'm an old man knowing I was successful at these four items. I want freedom to know I have enough, to be able to be fully present and enjoy each moment without worries.

That is success. You never fully get there, it is a process. We're in a world where eventually everything deteriorates and dies. But, at the same time, I hope I get closer to success every day.

---

1 http://bit.ly/jxlS1s

If there was a shortcut to success, what would it be? @kehindabajo

The best short cut to success is to avoid failure. Do what you can to avoid getting sick, avoid doubt, avoid vacillation, avoid being negligent to your responsibilities, avoid being dull (lacking any momentum), avoid being lazy (hard for me), avoid cravings that are unhealthy for you or impossible to achieve, try to avoid having misperceptions about what society tells you is TRUTH. It is not.

What are the antidotes to these obstacles to success? Tell the truth as much as you can. And harm nobody. That's the beginning. Then every day, save a life.

What is the sixth law of power and how important is it? @justinjmoses

When I answered this I was, and still am, assuming the question is referring to that book "*Power: The 48 Laws of Power.*" I don't like that book. I think many of the "laws" are about building yourself up at the expense of others.

Success is not a zero-sum game; else we would still be back in the dark ages. You are most successful when your one overriding thought is how can I bring the most success to others.

That's the one law of power that everyone needs.

But, I'll answer the question: the Sixth Law of Power in the book is to court attention wherever you possibly can.

This is not so bad, relative to some of the other "laws" in the book.

However, you can't court attention for the sake of courting attention. Everthing you do has to provide value. If you write a blog post, if you tweet, if you perform a service, deliver value. Don't even think of doing something without asking first, *"What value am I providing"?*

So, for instance, I'm courting attention by compiling this book. By doing the Twitter Q&A's, by writing blog-posts. I'm trying to court a lot of attention. Some of it is for ego purposes probably. Some of it is so people think of me when potential opportunities arise. I don't deny I have selfish purposes.

But first and foremost, deliver value. That really should be the sixth law of power. And then, if the value is real and helps people, attention happens automatically.

JOBS

Is it ever too late to escape from Corporate America? Even for a serious career change? @GoldenStLiberty

Absolutely not. In fact, if you are asking that question then you already know the answer.

Here's the thing about "Corporate America":

- Your boss usually sucks and someone eventually stabs you in the back. It's inevitable.
- Fluorescent lights (why are fluorescent lights so annoying?)
- Up to 50% of your income is taxed
- Between commuting and working it is usually a 10 to 11 hour a day process
- Your mind and creative abilities start to atrophy. And maybe you get out of shape.

- It's not safe. We used to think that Corporate America met safe, rising jobs, promotions, salaries, life savings, etc. 2008 showed us that was all a lie. Heck, 100,000 people lost their life savings when GM went bust. GM was the most solid company in the world 20 years ago. So don't count on any corporation to tuck you in bed at night and sing you a lullaby. Corporate America is not Mary Poppins, it's the Exorcist.

So if you even have a semblance of desire to get out of it, you must start planning your exit. You don't have to do it in a day. But set the forces in motion:

START COMING UP WITH IDEAS ABOUT WHAT ELSE YOU CAN DO. It might mean multiple streams of income instead of just one. It might mean freelance. But get your idea muscle in motion. You need to exercise it because it already atrophied. Ten ideas a day for six months and write down what all the next steps of each idea are. Eventually you will be an idea machine. The corporation will get scared because they will see it on you. This has happened to me. They will keep promoting you and raising your salary because they will be afraid to lose you. But they have already lost you.

WOW, THAT WAS A BIG POINT. I need another point here just to point that out.

IF YOU HAVE TO, GET READY TO DOWNSIZE. You don't need to live in NYC, for instance, if you're not going to be working at the big bank anymore. And cash is king. Don't buy a house. Save your cash.

MY OWN EXPERIENCE: I left corporate America working as a programmer at HBO in order to build a company making websites.[1] It was brutal at first. Then a few years later I had a job offer at a huge investment bank. No way suckers! I turned that down so I could have a miserable few years day trading for hedge funds until I built Stockpickr.com. Not every day of "life on your own" will be a happy one. But the challenges will be different and you

1 http://bit.ly/erAKRa

will be your own boss. And you might go broke. Who cares! At least you know you can do it again and again. Not everytime you have sex there are fireworks right over your house. But you still go back the next day and beg and plead for more (oh wait, maybe that's just me).

[See also, "10 Reasons You Need to Quit Your Job Right Now"[1]]

I have a trouble finding a job, although I got an MBA in US, worked in China for 7 years, trilingual, trying hard on networking.
@Jacquelinexu

Clearly you are qualified for anything. You can be a congresswoman or a janitor. You can be a hedge fund trader or a secretary for the vice-president of manufacturing at a local ball-bearings company. You can be a stewardess on Shanghai Air or you can be an expert on Chinese import-exports. Anything.

So why aren't people hiring you? It's a hard world out there. In a hard world the way to stand out is to help other people stand out and succeed. It's hard for them also.

Between your MBA and your 7 years in China you must know A LOT of people.

Here's what I would do if I were you:

- Every day, get your coffee, and start thinking about two people you can introduce to each other and why. How their lives would benefit if they met.

  Then introduce them. It will take about ten minutes. After 20 days you would've helped 40 people improve their lives. One of those people is going to have a job for you.

1 http://bit.ly/ipsmoi

Another idea. And this is one that I've seen applied repeatedly over the past two years and it's driven opportunities to many people:

- Organize a dinner. Be prepared to spend about $1000+ or find a sponsor for the dinner. Do it at a nice restaurant. Call it Chinese-American Business Awareness dinner. Invite everyone you can think of: include media, investors, business owners, and your colleagues from business school. Even get a speaker if you can.

  As the center of this, all the attention comes on you. This is the most powerful networking tool out there but many won't do it out of shyness or lack of interest in spending the money on paying for 30 bottles of wine, food, plus tip. But this will make you stand out for sure. When you are the source, all good things flow back to you.

- Blog every day about another person who has taken advantage of his or her Chinese-American knowledge and how valuable the intersection of that knowledge is. For instance, Robin Li was a lowly worker at Dow Jones in the US. Came up with a search engine idea. Felt it was too competitive here, so went back to China to create Baidu. Have some "big" stories (Robin Li) and some small stories, people we've never heard of. Again, you become the source. We all follow the source.

Try these for a while. Also try some of the ideas I suggest in "Nine Ways to Be a Super-Connector"

I wake up every morning and am positive for about 30 seconds and then the tick list of everything negative creeps in, suggestion?
@ScottVanEpps

I do this as well. Here's what I do:

LABEL EACH THOUGHT: "USEFUL", "NOT USEFUL." Try to do that for as long as you can. I recommend this in "The Power of Negative Thinking."[1] You'll find that a lot of those negative thoughts are "not useful" and you move on quickly. In fact, I just realized this second I was thinking of a not useful angry thought about something someone sent me on an email (usually the ones closest to you are the ones that know how to push your buttons) and I had to do the "not useful" thing a few times before continuing this answer.

UNDERSTAND THAT MOST THINGS YOU HAVE WORRIED ABOUT DIDN'T COME TRUE. I've worried about stuff for the past 15 years at 3 in the morning. Almost everything I ever worried about didn't come true, or, had a solution long before it became a problem. If you do the daily practice, and take care of the four basic areas of life it focuses on, you will be able to fight the problems long before they come to fruition.

ASSUME THE WORST CASE SCENARIO. What happens then? Really picture it. I know it's bad. But you will survive and move on. Sometimes the worst cases scenario is unimaginable. But if it doesn't involve our own death, we usually can figure it out and move on and we'll still laugh at a funny movie and the best we can to the people around us if they will still have us. And if they don't, then we go on to new adventures.

How do you do things you hate but have to do? @liewmomo

There are a couple of answers now that I think more of it.

- Each day limit the things you do that you hate. If you hate talking to your boss, for instance, then either talk less to your boss (no social chit-chat, no extra brown-nosing chats, etc.) or Quit Your Job.[2] If you don't want to go to a wedding then just don't go.

- If you absolutely have to do something you despise, then learn something from it. Sergey Brin says he can tell in a few sec-

---

1 http://www.jamesaltucher.com/2011/07/the-power-of-negative-thinking/

2 http://bit.ly/ipsmoi

onds of an interview if he is going to hire someone. But he can't just leave the interview. So he makes sure he learns at least one thing. I often don't want to go into New York City for meetings. But I always make sure there's at least one adventure along the way.

- Stop hating so much? There are two sides to the equation: there's the thing you "have to do" and there's the thing you "hate." In the above two items we deal with how you can change what you do. But can we also change what you hate? Why do you hate it? For everything you hate, can you list some positives? I hate going on a plane. But the positive is that I'll have an adventure in a new place. I hate when people make bad comments on any of my articles. But the positive is that I know I'm deeply affecting them and that something inside of them is forcing them to respond in a hateful way. Suddenly it becomes a pleasure to get these comments. I used to hate dating. But I knew eventually, with quantity, I would meet someone with quality.

How did you go from HBO to Hedge Funds? @Hamzah81

I worked at HBO and then I inappropriately hired myself to HBO's website. It was a success. Other companies started hiring me to do their websites because they wanted HBO's flavor. Eventually I had to quit HBO, had millions in revenues, and sold the company.

The company I sold to was for stock. That stock multiplied by 10 and I was able to sell a lot. Then, thinking I was a genius I bought every internet stock I could find and watched them all go to zero. I lost $15 million dollars. So I had to rebuild. I was depressed and losing my home.

I wrote software to take my emotions out of the equation. The software traded automatically. The basic idea is that when a stock fell 20% or more in a day, it was usually good for a 6% pop over the next few days. I tested this statistically and it worked for me throughout all of 2001 and 2002. I sent my ideas to a few hedge fund managers and they decided to trust me with their money in managed accounts.

Note: I had no experience making websites, no experience in TV, no experience in trading, and no experience in writing for financial media. But I did it anyway. Nobody was going to tell me not to. I would not have listened.

What balance should we have in life between: learning by reading or watching others / learning by doing? *@HarrisonAmy*

Always 50-50. For example, when I write, I read for 2-3 hours first, and then write for 2-3 hours. When I start a business, I read every book I can about successful entrepreneurs and I spend time networking as much as possible with other startup entrepreneurs.

Even when I was dating, I spent part of each day researching dating (i.e. sending out messages on dating services, for instance) thinking about how I can make a date better, etc. And then, of course, the other part of each day actually dating.

@HarrisonAmy then asked me how I know when I'm off balance.

The way I know is if I have a hard time coming up with new ideas. If I feel the "flow" is missing. I spend part of each day trying to come up with ideas for myself on whatever I'm interested in. If I'm too distracted or not thinking of enough good ideas then I know I'm off balance.

Is being married to work really a bad thing when you are young. Do I really have a lot of time to find my life partner? *@niketdesai*

It's very important to be married to work when you are young. To develop ideas and have a passion that takes you beyond the competition (the rest of society). Too many people spend their 20s chasing simple and easy pleasures without regard to their own health and without regard to building up so that later in life they can pursue more fruitful pursuits.

Also, looking at the divorce rate of people who are married in their 20s its often better to be married to your work than to be married to a human.

What are your tips for interviewing? I always seem to choke up and get performance anxiety. @unionkane

Before an interview:

PREPARE. Know everything you can about the history of the business you are interviewing for. How did it start? What is the backgrounds of the founders? What were the goals of the business? How have they changed? When has the business faltered in the past? With any large company you can always find this out. Make sure you do.

BECOME THE COMPANY. In a science fiction sense you want to mind-meld with the company. It's as if you were the company so the ideas you start to come up with are ideas that will better the company. This will shine through in the interview.

BOOST YOUR CONFIDENCE WITH EXTRA KNOWLEDGE. If you are interviewing for a smaller company it might not be so easy to do the above, but you can always know the competitors. Be familiar with the ups and downs in the industry.

Performance anxiety in an interview is similar to anxiety in any performance – it is 100% related to low confidence. You build confidence through knowledge and practice.

VISUALIZE. Before the interview, visualize the entire interview in your head. Bring up all the points you studied about the industry. Imagine yourself talking about what your role will be. Bring up ideas you have. Play with it, see yourself doing great. Make it fun, visualize hearing an offer beyond your wildest dreams, make it big, make it successful, then let it all go.

EXCERSISE. This reduces anxiety and helps you focus. The one draw-back is that it could make you tired. Therefore, once you exercise, build the mind muscles back up by coming up with 10 ideas for the business. Brand new ideas, ones you have not thought of before. Even if it's interviewing to work as a shoe store salesman, make sure you understand every brand out there, how the store can use social media to drive customers, etc.

GOOGLE IT. You can usually get the names of the people you are going to meet in the interview process. Of course, use Google to find out everything about them. Again, the overriding consideration is that knowledge builds confidence which reduces anxiety. Exercise also reduces anxiety.

FINALLY, SURRENDER. It is very important to have a feeling of "Okay, I've done all I can. It's in your hands now. Whatever will be will be, I trust that what is best for all concerned will be the outcome.

Having a feeling of surrender and humility, and a sense that there's a higher power (even if you call it something as silly as "The Force") will help reduce anxiety.

NOW GO GET THE JOB. Don't think about the past (fired from prior jobs) or the future (if I don't get this job then I'm lost). These are "not useful" thoughts. Try to catch yourself in the middle of a not-useful thought (it takes practice) and see if you can replace it with its opposite. Stay rooted in the present moment, flow with it.

How do you get so much energy to do the things you do? @yoda_2little

Energy is a bit overrated. The key thing is to spend as little energy as possible and still get things done. Why would you want to spend little energy? Because everything you do in the outside world gives you little time to tend to the gardens that are inside your world, inside your mind, inside your body.

So the first thing is to spend less energy digesting food. Skip dinner (so your body is not trying to digest when you sleep), go to sleep early, don't expose yourself to news, avoid pop culture, don't drink alcohol, try to only be around the people you love, and have a sense of surrender and gratitude.

This may seem like you are sterilizing your life. But it's quite the opposite. When you have leftover energy to do whatever you want, then you have more possibilities than ever.

Sometimes I can pull this off. Sometimes I can't. But I'm always trying.

Been a stay at home housewife for 8 years and want to go back to work badly but feel defeated and hopeless about finding a job. How do I get out of funk? @mainlinewife

I obviously do not have direct experience with this but, that doesn't stop me from offering advice. First off, being a "stay at home housewife" seems embedded in how you view yourself. Your twitter handle is "mainlinewife" and your "name" associated with the handle is "Main Line Housewife."

We need to break you free from the identity you have created for yourself, from the cage you have put yourself in, from the boundaries you have personally drawn around you, like a kid playing with chalk on the playground during recess: *"Nobody can walk in these lines!"*

Second, congratulations on everything you've done. Obviously spending eight years devoted to raising children is a heroic and underrated task in our society. People shower credit on Mark Zuckerberg and make movies about him but the blood, sweat, and tears of making a brand new human being a responsible member of society is often forgotten.

Now back to your question, it takes work to get back into the job world. You need the confidence, the health, the idea engine, the spiritual engine, all working for you again. The idea muscles atrophy as quickly as any other muscle.

Most important: you need to exercise every day. And you need to write ideas down every day. Write ten ideas a day, about anything under the sun: ideas for jobs you can do, ideas for how you can help people, ideas for articles you can write, specific ideas on businesses you can start.

Assume that for one month you will only come up with bad ideas. That's ok. But give it three to six months and everything will be different. Particularly if your other relationships are more or less smooth, and physically you stay/get in shape. The key is to not lapse back into thinking, *"Damn, I can't do this. I'm just a housewife."* In which case, follow the advice in "Being Unpredictable Will Free You."[1]

Find a moment today to finger-paint. Or swim. Or take a walk by yourself. Or respondto an email from 1999. Do something that will take you out of your normal routine for 2 minutes. That's all it takes. What happens then? Who knows? The miraculous.

How do you know when the time is right to take the plunge, quit your job and focus on your own business? What about family risks? *@adamclay211*

What is a risk? I met someone the other day who worked for 38 years at GM. He was a middle-manager so he had no golden parachute (he wasn't a high level executive) and he had no bronze parachute (he wasn't a union member). Net result: he lost his life savings, his job, his savings.

There is no corporate safety. The risk to your family is you becoming inbred in your corporate job. You must leave, just as I recom-

1 http://www.jamesaltucher.com/2011/11/being-unpredictable-will-free-you/

mend in the post "10 Reasons You Have to Quit Your Job Right Now!"[1]

That said, don't go crazy. Make sure you are smart and jumping to something better than you are leaving.

If you are going to a startup, you are investing not cash (which comes and goes), but your entire life, your dreams, your skill sets, your soul. In other words, do your due diligence.

Here's a sample checklist:

- Talk to clients. Are they happy?

- What are the backgrounds of the heads of sales?

- Has the CEO built and sold a business before and taken care of his employees in the process?

- Does the company have at least 1 year's cash?

- What are their plans for future rounds of fundraising?

- Who are the current investors on the board? Do they have deep pockets to keep funding the company?

- Is the company squarely positioned in what you feel is a strong demographic trend?

- Has the company proven its flexibility (i.e. has it already had a chance to learn from its mistakes)

1 http://bit.ly/fpBXNZ

GOING BROKE

What did you do to make money after you went broke? @ScottEPowers

I did several things:

DOWNSIZED. I had to sell my house. I severely downsized. I went from a 4,500 square foot penthouse to a 1,400 square foot house 70 miles north and I cut my expenses by 75%.

I HAD TO GET IN SHAPE. I worked out every day, I emotionally stopped dealing with people who were dragging me down, I made lists of ideas every day, and I either meditated or read from various spiritual or inspirational texts each day. I knew it was going to be a tough battle to climb back up so I did everything I could to prepare.

IMMEDIATELY STARTED WRITING ABOUT FINANCE TO GENERATE INCOME. Within a few months I had a book deal and I was writing for TheStreet.com and The Financial Times. Back then it was still possible to make money by writing.

I was also day-trading and doing well back then (2002-05). I don't think day trading is practical now but it was then.

I STARTED TRADING FOR HEDGE FUNDS then I started helping people sell their companies, then I started a fund of hedge funds. One day at the time, as the ideas I wrote began to flourish I got back into the game.

I STARTED A COMPANY: STOCKPICKR.COM[1] which I sold to TheStreet.com. There was a six year period where nobody was paying my salary and I had to hustle for every dollar. But that proved to me that no matter how bad the economy gets, if you're the one eyed man (the optimist) in the land of the blind (the pes-

1 http://bit.ly/qV3Q5E

simists) then you will find the ways to make money even if we are in a Depression.

Have you ever given up on yourself? @bluenextbear

Yes, this is a perpetual problem I have, and maybe many people have: I give up on myself every day. I wake up, and I have to make sure my first thoughts are not negative thoughts. I get angry. And anger is just a small shade on the spectrum of emotions away from fear. So I usually get scared next.[1] Then I have to go to the bathroom. Fast.

But when I'm done with that, the key is how to get back on track. I try to practice an ongoing meditation, labeling thoughts as I catch them: "useful" or "not useful." Any anger or fear thoughts or thoughts of, "I can't do this" go in the "not useful" bucket. Then I begin my normal practices of the day. Exercising the idea muscle, writing, exercising. And so on.

Every day is a battle. Even if you have confidence one day, there are so many forces in the world (media, news, pop culture, family, enemies, bosses, colleagues, etc. etc. etc.) that are trying to bring you down that you need in your tool chest a daily method of performing surgery on yourself so that if you do give up, even if it's just for a moment, you have a way of coming back from the abyss.

In a black hole there's something called the event horizon. Once you enter that perimeter there is no escape and you are sucked into the black hole. There is no way possible for anything to comeback once it's in that zone. The same thing applies when giving up on yourself. You have to pull yourself back before you are sucked into that zone. Don't entertain it, don't dance with it, and don't feed that feeling. You must say "not useful" and move on. Continue with the incremental implementation of your plan, discussed above.

---

1 http://bit.ly/09MBAx

OPTIMISM

Do you think optimism and being positive even if you fail, and start again, and fail will make you succeed?
@catalin357

This is a trick question because the answer is both yes and no.

You need "rational optimism." If I say to myself, *"damn, I failed to make that time travel machine but I'm optimistic my next try will be it!"* then I'm doomed to fail.

How do you be a rational optimist?

BE REALISTIC. It's like the question where I describe coming up with ideas. Make sure you have realistic ideas, make sure you have a concrete next step, make sure you have an idea in your mind how you can get your first customers and users. If you can get a commitment for a customer even before you build, then that is the best scenario.

UNDERSTAND THAT SOME THINGS ARE OUT OF YOUR CONTROL. Having a sense of surrender, *"okay, I did all I could. It's in your hands now"* will help you to have an optimistic, flexible, and persistent outlook on life. If you just say, *"Ugh, I did everything I could and I failed and now that's it"* then of course, that's it!

WHO IS THE YOU IN: *"IT'S IN YOUR HANDS NOW"*? It might be your own creativity and flexibility that wants to get out and help you on your next idea. That creativity is a sleeping monster and it never gets smaller if you keep feeding it, nurturing it, loving it, taking care of it. Persistence in developing that creativity will make you better at execution, better at idea generation, and more optimistic (simply because over time you will be more confident that you can always awaken it). Creativity becomes your loving friend instead of your enemy. And optimism, creativity, and persistence are all close siblings that want to play together as much as possible.

MONEY

With Europe about to default, high employment, gold (the ultimate fear metal) on the rise, why should anyone still be bullish?
@ginger_gal

FACT: right now the top 5 banks in the US have 3% exposure to European debt. (How can this be? Because China is buying up all the European debt in their attempt to take over the financial planet.

In 1981 all of South America was in default. The top 5 banks in the US had 263% exposure to their debt. We had 17% inflation/ bond yields. Millions of jobs were being lost because of the high rates and inflation. And we had the Soviet Union with thousands of hydrogen bombs pointed at your home. Not to mention the revolution in Iran, unrest in India, Pakistan, Israel, etc.

And yet what happened: a two decade boom?

Ignore world politics, ignore the government statistics, ignore the headlines which try to make you scared, ignore the pundits who sell newsletters based on fear and greed.

They are all out to scam you. If you are putting your hopes and future happiness on the thought that the world is going to end you're going to be dead wrong.

What would be your strategy to get wealthy? @djmainevent

I think a lot of people get lucky on the road to wealth. They build some company in a hot space, and they sell it for an ungodly high number. Think Bebo, which got bought by AOL for a billion and then sold for $10 million a year or so later. Those founders got fabulously wealthy.

But for the rest of us that won't happen.

The real way to get wealth is to find a customer and perform a service for that customer. Then repeat. My first company found a customer (a company that needed a website) and built the website for that customer. Then we found another customer and built that website. And word of mouth spread and before you knew it we were making websites for dozens of companies. I also always made sure I delivered at least one extra feature that the company didn't ask for.

One way to get a customer is to help other companies get customers and you charge for that service. If you live by a bunch of gyms, put up Facebook ads for those gyms and then charge them for every customer that walks through the door, for instance.

But, you must get the idea muscle in shape. The idea muscle is like any other muscle. Within 2-3 weeks of no use it atrophies. If you don't use your legs for two weeks you won't be able to work. Same thing here.

So every day get to work. Come up with ideas. For yourself, for others, for other companies. Give it a few weeks before you suspect that you might be in shape. Then a few months before you're ready to start sharing your ideas.

At this point your ideas will be good enough to help other people make money. When you make other people make money, then you will make money. Then you repeat that and it's a business.

Don't forget that when you come up with an idea, the idea is no good unless you also have the "next step" and perhaps even the next step after that. Anyone can come up with the idea: I want to set up a small airline between every city in the New York/Connecticut region. But what would the next steps be? Can you do them? This is a gut check to make sure your idea is realistic enough to pursue, whether it's for yourself or others.

Is greed good?
@tradefast

The phrase "greed is good" has become a cliché for periods of excess like the 80s or the mid 00s, where real characters like Ivan Boesky or fictional characters like Gordon Gekko use it as an excuse for their own illegal activities.

However, don't believe the hype. Don't just watch TV or read the newspaper headlines and nod your head with everyone else: "They are all out to get me with their stupid greed."

I have greed to make money. I want to feed my family. I want them to have shelter. I want to be able to afford if they get sick. Furthermore, I might want to start new companies, or create new jobs, or work on other ideas and innovations instead of working as a salesclerk in the Verizon store (as the guy who caught Derek Jeter's ball did, and he then handed the ball back for free instead of taking the potential $250,000 offered).

Greed is good if you are good.

BEING STUCKED

How Can I Get Un-Stucked? Asked privately via comments.

A lot of people get stuck. They don't like where they are at. They don't know how to move forward. They don't know how to shake things up. I don't know if this is true but one time a friend of mine told me (he got his PHD at the age of 15 so I believed everything he told me about science) that the way Bic makes lighters is by putting all the parts in a machine and then the machine shakes until the parts somehow all fit together into lighters and the lighters start falling out.

I don't know if this is true. But I love the idea.

A lot of people are stuck. I know this because I get emails that start, *"I'm stuck."* So how to get "unstuck." Put all your parts in a machine. Start shaking.

Even when I was stuck I couldn't accurately say I had specific complaints. I had an ok job, good boss, ok colleagues, easy responsibilities. Summers were easy when everyone took a vacation (and on that note: how bad are vacations? Much better when you get to sit around and do nothing than go off to Hawaii or Alaska, battle airplanes, hotels, "hiking" (ugh!), feeding kids, etc). So what was my problem?

Nothing was my problem. It's ok to be stuck. Nobody will ever blame you for it. But you'll get less and less happy. Then things start to happen that you didn't intend, in order to get you unstuck. Maybe you have an affair to mix things up. Maybe you steal a little from the office. Maybe you start to cut corners at work because you've been there long enough you know you can let things slide. You start gossiping too much about the other people. You begin the arduous process of backstabbing to rise up in a world that will tease you into thinking that's how you get unstuck.

But it isn't. And being stuck has its consequences. Here's the ten step guide to being unstuck:

LIST YOUR ROUTINE. Don't leave a single detail out. When you are stuck it means you have a rigid routine that rarely changes. Here was part of my routine: Wake up, brush teeth, wait for cold subway, ride subway, get a donut and coffee, go to cubicle without anyone seeing me, log onto email, read stuff on the web, play a game of chess, make my list of things to do, start programming... flirt... gossip... kiss-ass... lunch... coffee break... chess break... dinner... shoot pool..., etc. I had about 50 things on my "Routine List." Put 60 if you can.

CHANGE ONE THING: in the routine. The idea is to only change one thing at a time. Don't be too hard on yourself. One thing. And don't do the exact opposite. Just avoid the item in the routine you want to change. Maybe, don't go straight to work. Go to the library. Or wake up one hour early and read a book. Or jog around the block even if you have never jogged before. Or don't read your emails this morning. Or completely stop gossiping. Or sit with different people at lunch. Over time, how many things on your routine list can you change? Half? All of it? Make it a daily challenge. Break your record. Break my record.

INSTEAD OF WRITING A TO-DO LIST WRITE A "THINGS I DID" LIST AT THE END OF THE DAY. In fact, start to reverse your routine. Read emails at the end of the day. Have dinner for breakfast. Breafast for dinner.

FIND ONE THING YOU WERE PASSIONATE ABOUT AS A KID: spend an hour researching what has happened since. For instance, I was passionate about Jacques Cousteau for about a month as a kid. What ever happened to that guy? I couldn't tell you right now if he was dead or alive or buried in some sex scandal. He put out a bunch of books about what goes on underwater. What's happened since? Why do this? You were a kid for 18 years. There were probably many things that you were passionate about. Even if it was as silly as some cartoon show. Each thing you find out about is something new you learn now. And you might find things you are still passionate about.

NETWORK: Every day find one person to reach out to and stay in touch with. An old high school friend. A guy you randomly spoke to on the subway. The guy on the elevator. Go out to lunch with this person. Learn about his life. Interview him. You need to find out what other routines are like. Maybe someone will give you an idea you haven't thought of. We are all very very afraid to break out of our routines. I am also. I recently agreed to do a media appearance simply because I was afraid if I said "no" then the people there would not like me. Claudia begged me not to do it. I did it anyway. She was right. I was afraid to break out of my routine. But networking that day would've probably put me more in touch with people who liked me than doing that media appearance did. Again, return the email from 2005 that you never returned. Write a letter to your boss's boss's boss's boss and tell him what you really think about the company's strategy in Kansas.

CREATE. I can tell by the emails I get that most people would rather create something than be a part of the robotic routine. How can you create if you have no time or if you have never done it before? Simple! Don't worry about either of those things. On the subway write a 4 line poem. Buy a set of watercolors in the drug store and finger paint for ten minutes before you go to sleep. Don't write a things to do list or a things you did list. Write a "things I wish I did today" list. Make up stuff for that list. I wish a UFO picked me up, took me to Andromeda, and then took me home for dinner. Its your wish list for the day that just happened. It's all over. So you can wish for anything. It didn't happen. You are making stuff up. You're creating.

HERE IS ANOTHER THING: FOLLOW SOMEONE. I love doing this! Pick a random person and just follow them for fifteen minutes. You're an evil spy! Then you can see their routine. Make sure they don't see you follow them. [See, "Nine Ways to Light Your Creativity On Fire."[1]]

---

1 http://www.jamesaltucher.com/2011/08/nine-ways-to-light-your-creativity-on-fire/

DAILY PRACTICE. I'm a broken record already. Here's why the Daily Practice I recommend works: (note: what this is my personal belief about how the world and universe is set up. You don't have to believe it. But I know it works for me). I firmly believe we have four bodies and most of the time we are neglecting at least 2 or 3 of them if not all 4. If you neglect your physical body, you start to have stomach disorders, you get sick more frequently, you eventually die younger or at least have a painful, unpleasant life. Guess what!? The same thing happens if you neglect your emotional body. Or mental body. Or spiritual body.

And it's even bigger than that. In your physical body (in all 4) there's blood that hooks everything up. If the blood is not working, oxygen is not getting to the different parts of your body. You might have to breathe faster then, or you might breathe irregularly, or worse: if oxygen doesn't get to the heart or the brain then you have a heart attack or stroke. If oxygen doesn't get properly to your cells you get cancer. The same thing happens in all four bodies. BUT, it's not only that: there's a blood that connects up each body. If they aren't all in sync then that blood flow starts to break down.

I know people don't care about all four bodies. They say to me, *"I love the idea muscle idea."* Or, "I like your thoughts but don't really think much about spirituality." If ALL FOUR BODIES are not in harmony with each other then they being to break down. Then they start letting crappy people into their lives. Or they start being unable to execute on good ideas. Or they get sick. Whatever. Many people don't like some words. Like "spiritual." Call it something else then.

And don't believe me at all on this. I'm making it all up after all. But I know, for me, this is what works. I can't break out of a routine, any routine, unless I am following this advice. So I know it works for me. And I know it works for the people who read my writing because I get their emails. I've gotten well over 1000 emails so far on how people's lives have changed. I'm not saying this because I am trying to sell you anything. I'm not selling anything at all. In fact, better for me to "succeed" if less people follow my advice. But whatever, it works for me.

BUY ALL MY BOOKS. Ha-ha. I'm just kidding. I just told you I'm not selling anything. But, seriously, buy my last book.

WHAT ARE YOU AFRAID OF? Sometimes a "routine" is a person. I wake up..did she write me? ...its 11a.m ...has she called? ... did she say she loved me yesterday? ...how come she didn't make plans yet for this weekend with me ...she said she would be here at 7 but she hasn't even called and its 8 ...etc. Maybe this routine is particular to me. But ask: why might I have a routine like that (in the past). List your reasons: fear of being alone. A parent telling me I was disgusting when I was youger. Experiences of other women cheating if its 8 and they said 7.

Fear that I will *"never meet someone like her again"* (a statement which is always said but never true). Sexual obsession. Love addiction. On an on.

You break the routine by being aware of the fears: I'll never get a job this good again. I'll fail as an entrepreneur. I'll run out of money and have to move. I don't know any rich people to help me. Excuse after excuse of why you shouldn't break your routine.

List all of those excuses. Think about them. Think of the opposite *("well, I've always met a girl within six months after a big breakup so I will probably meet one again"* or, *"I haven't lived in a homeless shelter yet so odds are I won't this time.")*

But I can't change them!? You might say. *"I really want this girl!"* Or... *"I really might go broke!"* That's ok. Think them.

Here's how you wither them away, like the water against a rock metaphor:

1. BECOME AWARE OF THE EXCUSES

2. FIGURE OUT WHY THEY EXIST. What part of your psychological timeline do they come from?

3. WHERE IN YOUR BODY DO YOU FEEL PAIN WHEN YOU THINK OF THEM? Just think about that.

4. WHAT'S THE REVERSE OF THAT FEAR. I really had to say to myself, *"I will meet a woman. I will fall in love with if I leave this girl."* I had to say it over and over. If I didn't say it, I never would've left the girl. I never would've met the right girl. If you don't say it, you won't believe it. I had to say, *"if I start a company I won't go broke."*

5. VISUALIZE now what you just said in part "4." Lie down. Put your hands by your side. Take ten deep breaths. And really visualize the situation. You will meet the girl. Your business will be a success.

You might say, *"that's sort of new agey."* Ok. Don't do it then. All I'm saying is: this is how I broke my routines. All of them. Every time. Even micro-routines.

Then repeat from "i" tomorrow.

I eventually climbed out of bed and told my boss I quit. He said, *"Can you please wait until I get back from vacation in 3 weeks?"* I said *"no"* and sent in my resignation. I eventually stopped calling back "the girl" when it was clear she didn't like me. Eventually I also stopped gossiping about the people who clearly hated me. I never ended up in a homeless shelter despite repeated attempts for the universe to put me there.

PERFECTIONISM

How do you deal with perfection? Many times I feel I can't execute ideas until I know it 100%.
@socialhotchoco

Perfectionism only leads to eventual shame or regret. Nobody is perfect, and there's always the chance of the unknown occurring in every work. And, when the perfectionist loses control of an event, project, business, etc. then what happens? Shame results. Embarrassment with colleagues, friends, bosses, investors, and family.

A very public example is Madoff. At some point he started his hedge fund and lost some money. He was a perfectionist. He couldn't handle telling people that he lost money. Everyone thought he was an investment genius. The result: a massive Ponzi scheme as he attempted to cover up his imperfections and still be the "genius" everyone thought he was.

So my advice: if you have an idea for a project: Start it. Start it right now. Spec out the minimal features you need, hire a programmer (use Scriptlance), or find a customer, and just get started. Even if you are not 100% ready.

As an example: I have an idea for a novel. I don't have the full plot outlined. I don't even know if I will have the time to finish. But today I'm going to start it. I'll write just 500 words for it. It doesn't have to be perfect (that's what rewriting is for), but we'll see what happens.

How do I deal with anxiety about not being perfect at everything I do?
@paramkamal

Giving yourself permission to be imperfect is the key to all flexibility and success. Think of the first time you tried to touch your toes while your knees were straight. You couldn't do it. Too inflexible.

With time, you get a millimeter closer each day. Then it's painful. But with time, you wiggle into it. Now you go for more. You put your hands on your feet. You twist towards the ceiling. You open up your muscles. You open up your mind. But it all started with small imperfections that you conquered day by day.

GOALS AND ADVICE

Words of advice someone said to you that changed your life?
@adriennetran

I had a real hard time with this at first. Most of the people who have "mentored" me I ultimately got distanced from for a variety of reasons. [See, "The Worst Boss I've Ever Had"[1]]

But here's a couple of things that people have said to me that I have not forgotten:

"Try to improve every day" (Jim Cramer told me that one.[2])

"Focus on today only" (Claudia told me that one when I was worrying about a hypothetical event that could happen two years from now)

"I'm only worried about what's in my pocket, not what's in your pocket" (a good way to focus on your own needs and finances and not be obsessed with the mythical Jones family we always try to keep up with. Yitz told me that one.[3])

1 http://bit.ly/oS8lYT
2 http://bit.ly/hOrF87
3 http://bit.ly/lvBeW2

"Always be honest" (my dad taught me that one, the hard way.[1])

Unfortunately, most other things I've had to learn on my own.

How important is having a plan if you want to get anywhere in life?
@djmainevent

It is very important to have a plan. For instance, let's say you want to be able to bench press 200 lbs. (I'm making this up, obviously. I never want to be able to bench press that). You won't get there randomly. You first come up with the goal ("bench press 200 lbs") and then with that goal in hand you know every day how you can slightly improve to meet that goal. How you can change your diet (more protein!), how you can get to a gym, what increments you need to take in order to bench 200 lbs, which muscles need to improve (there's a billion little muscles around the shoulder that have to be worked on with different machines, etc). And so on.

I have about 8 goals that I've written down for 2012. I look at them every day. The goals might change. I might not stick with them. Or I might decide halfway through that I'm only going to focus on 4 of them. But each day I come up with the plan for that day that makes incremental improvement on all 8 goals. Those incremental improvements compound in your life exponentially the way money in a bank accumulating interest does. Before you know it, you are rich in the sense that you've achieved your plan. But without the plan, you are just flaying in the dark, with no money in your mental bank.

Who do you turn to for advice?
@bondtrader83

It's important to have someone you can trust and that, in just about any situation, you can turn to for advice. It's no wonder that many great businesses are started by two people: Google, Microsoft, Apple. For me, I turn to Claudia (Claudiayoga.com) when I most need advice.

---

1 http://bit.ly/qNWbHD

What would you tell the 17 year old you if you got the chance?
@JessWhat

When I was 17 all I thought about was sex, money, and chess. What an idiot. And I had acne. I don't even have any pictures of myself at 17. I'm so disgusted with what I was. But... There was this book on my parent's bookshelf when I was a kid. I constantly would thumb through it. It had a lot of stuff about sex in it. So that turned me on. But I think I ignored the title and what it meant. This is what I would tell myself if I could communicate to my 17 year old self.

Should we take advice from others?
@ibrute

Never! And that includes all the advice I am giving or have ever given.

This seems like an odd answer. I'm giving advice here after all. I spend an hour answering questions on Twitter on Thursdays. Then I summarize them as posts. Not to mention all my other posts I write. Plus the thousands of hours spent on writing books. Don't I think people should take my advice? Do I have such a low opinion of myself that I think people should ignore me?

In the last four paragraphs of *"I Was Blind But Now I See"* I say:

Seeing is realizing that all the wealth and success in the world is ours for the taking once we've build the foundations within, the true freedom that lets us see the reality and the myths around us for what they are.

It is questioning everything we do and the intentions behind them.

It is realizing that sometimes our intentions have a lot of strings attached and that not being honest is expensive. Very expensive. These techniques, these ideas, I've learned the hard way. I've succeeded on traditional terms. I've failed on very traditional terms.

I've been brainwashed by the Zombie Recruitment Machine. But I've also used the techniques in this book to now create success for myself. Nothing I suggest in this book is without decades of exploration and experimentation. Don't take my word for it.

Now is the time for you to take your own journey. To see the world. To figure out what you truly want, find success, wealth, freedom, happiness, and live the life you always knew you were meant to live. Enjoy.

What is one small way to improve my day to day routine? I need to add another positive piece to the puzzle? @randyaaron

THE DAILY PRACTICE,[1] which gives advice on how to make improvements physically, emotionally, mentally, and spiritually.

DEVELOPING YOUR GRATITUDE MUSCLE.[2] This is perhaps the easiest and most useful meditation: spend just two minutes thinking of the people in your life you are grateful for. Even better, pick one out from the distant past and reach out and tell them you are grateful.

NINE WAYS TO LIGHT YOUR CREATIVITY ON FIRE.[3]

Here are the nine ways: 1. List things. 2. Turn upside down. 3. Combine ideas (very important. Ideas mate with each other). 4. Study new technology. 5. Connect people. 6. Make something. Even if you don't have any creative skills, finger paint at the very least. It will awaken neurons you didn't know you had. 7. Leave. Go on a Staycation. Take yourself out on a date. Go someplace you've never been before in your own town. Ride on a swing. 8. Virtually leave. In the post I give links to some websites that I use sometimes to kick start my creativity. 9. Seek HELP.

1 http://bit.ly/fuiRS9
2 http://bit.ly/pY3Qvs
3 http://bit.ly/nOPi16

What's your dream? What's your biggest goal in life? @valuewalk

My biggest goal is to have much fewer goals. This sounds sort of clichéd but it's true. Goals are stressful. Let's say your goal is to have $100 million. That's hard! It's stressful to accomplish. It requires a lot of work. And then the question is: is it really necessary to have $100 million to be happy?

Or let's say my goal is to publish a novel? That's hard also! It will take time away from my kids, from my wife. It's hard to make money writing fiction (you have to be either lucky, super-talented, or super prolific, or all of the above) so you end up having to market yourself a lot, which is stressful.

We all have to support our families. But when that goal is largely accomplished to the best of our abilities, what other goals should we have? I don't want to lie around watching TV all day. But I guess if you constantly seek to improve yourself physically, emotionally, mentally, spiritually, then that's the best goal to have because that's the goal that will keep you happy, and help those around you, and turn you into an idea/innovation machine that will inspire others.

I hope I can get to a point where that's my only goal. Instead, I probably have too many "extra" goals that are nothing but baggage I have to carry around all the time.

Someone also asked: If you had to choose between physical health and mental health, what would you choose?

The answer (and I hope I never have to make that choice) is physical health. The reason is: you want high quality of life into your elder years. This gives you as much time and energy as possible to pursue the other three types of health I talk about. That said, they are all linked (stress will decrease your physical health, for instance). And physical health and exercise will help to keep you mentally balanced.

How do you learn to think on your feet? @socialhotchoco

Things always go wrong. All the time. When I was selling my first company, everything went wrong. We lost clients. Our landlord refused to give approval. We forget to get health insurance for our employees (and we had to admit that to our buyer), we were going bankrupt if the acquisition didn't close within a month.

But every problem has a solution. Your mind has to be as flexible as possible. Some people say, *"The mind gets flexible through meditation."* I find that only works for a few people. Not everyone can start off sitting for an hour a day and not get totally bored or fall asleep. Meditation is not really meant for most people (this is my opinion).

But you can train your mind to be flexible and to think fast. When I exercise muscles, I exercise until I hurt. Until I sweat. Until I know the next day I'm going to be sore. Otherwise the exercise doesn't work.

It is the same thing with the mind. You have to every day exercise it until it hurts. Until is sore the next day. Until you can't go on any further but you know you have to if you want your idea muscles to be working. Idea muscles atrophy. You need to exercise them every day to build them back up. The benefits:

- You will be able to think on your feet regardless of what problem comes up

- You will become an idea machine

- Other people with ideas will be attracted to you. Ideas want to mate. They want to give birth to new ideas. So people who have the idea muscles sharpened will become evolutionarily attracted to you to get new ideas born.

Just start with this: every day take a waiter's pad and write down ten ideas. Then, with each idea, come up with the next two steps of how to get that idea done. If it's a book idea, write the outline. If it's a chapter idea, write down what the chapter is about. If it's a business idea, write down some initial customers, or what the next step is on getting the idea implemented. Hurt your head. Keep thinking on each idea until you have to stop and say, *"ugh, this hurts to push any more on this idea."* Do that for six months.

Then you join the ranks of the Idea Machines.

For a 30 year old, no debt, no kid, likes job, has unneeded $100,000 in bank earning 1%. Leave it there long term or into VTI (the broadly diversified stock market)? @optradero

Holy shit, I'm jealous of you. Thirty years old, no responsibilities, and $100,000 in the bank. Do you know how lucky you are?

So let's see, you have two choices:

One, put it in the bank and never worry about it.

Two, put it in the stock market where it can either go up 6% on average or some years go down 30%. Hmm.

Why even consider option two? What would you have earned last year, for instance? Zero. After going 20% down at points. What a roller coaster when you could have just slept easy.

Cash is king. If I were you, I'd stuff it under the mattress. Don't even put it in a bank that could go under. Use some non-bank like Fidelity.

"No worries," should be your slogan. And when the time is right, take $1,000-2,000 and start your own business. If that doesn't work, then take another $1,000 and start another business. And keep trying.

People get trigger happy when they have a loaded gun. They want to fire it. But the best gun is the one that stays loaded. Don't risk your life for an extra ten cents.

Give me one piece of killer advice that I can use daily to make it a successful 2012
@AJBoom

If a gun was to my head and I had to give one piece of advice (hard for me: I'm like a vomitorium of advice) it would be:

Spend more time with people who love you. You can do this at home, work, on the internet, wherever.

Corollary: spend less time with people who don't love you.

By the way, this advice was given to me by Tucker Max, author of the book *"Assholes Finish First."*

COLLEGE

Should I follow my lifelong dream or go to college?
@himynameissteev

My stance on college is very clear. Some people might say that your dream will always be there but you might as well have college to fall back on.

Actually, the reverse is true. Your dream might not always be there (college has a way of dampening dreams) and college is no longer there to fall back on.

Going to college means:

- Graduating with enormous debt. You become a debt slave.

- Taking five years out of your life to get a piece of paper with your name on it.

- Spending five years NOT pursuing the things you are truly interested in. Life is short. 5 years could be 10% of your life. Why waste this valuable time?

Pursue the dream first. Pursue it in every way possible. Throw yourself into it because when you are at the ages of 18-22, that is when you have the passion and energy to try things. And besides, nobody is expecting much from you anyway (other than expecting you to go to college).

Later you can change your mind. You can always change your mind. But if you consistently make it a habit to put dreams on hold, the only thing that's left is nightmares.

You said don't go to college, may I know why? @CashN1n9

I've written many articles and posts on this, and I've had at least seven death threats on this topic. Here's one of my posts.[1] Here's one of the death threats.[2]

Let me try to summarize quickly:

- Student loan debt is higher than ever. Tuitions have risen even higher than health care costs since I went to college. So why isn't there a national discussion on this?

- Kids take the money and we all know what they do those four years. Don't deny it!

1 http://www.jamesaltucher.com/2011/01/10-more-reasons-why-parents-should-not-send-their-kids-to-college/

2 http://www.jamesaltucher.com/2011/02/why-does-taylor-northcutt-want-to-kill-me/

- They've just spent 12 years behind a desk listening to boring teachers and taking tests. Why don't you let them try one of these eight alternative.[1]

- There's a big stat: kids with college degrees make more money. Unfortunately anyone who took statistics 101 knows the flaw in this statistic. Can you explain?

Why do you often encourage people to drop out of school, when you graduated from a good college with a respectable degree?
@oliverg12

Obviously this is a hostile question. My assumption is that the real statement this person is making is: you don't want other people to accrue the other benefits you've accrued. You want to keep people down.

So, several answers:

- I went to college so that gives me experience on what college is really about. Would you rather have someone who didn't go to college tell kids not to go to college? In which case, there are also many examples.

- College now is different than when I was a kid. The most important difference: student loan debt is now so high that it exceeds credit card debt for the first time ever. Inflation has gone up 3-fold in the past 40 years, healthcare costs have gone up 5-fold, and tuitions for college have gone up 10-fold. How is this fair?

- People say, well, college students make more money than non-college students. This statement suffers from selection bias. The "type of people" who went to college twenty years ago certainly make more than the type of people who chose not to go to college twenty year ago. That's a completely different statement and more correct.

---

1 http://bit.ly/iewfpx

If you had a very intelligent child entering college today, what major and language skills would you recommend?
@goldfo100

Here's the problem, in a nutshell, with entering college – you are going to be with the same people you spent the past 12 years with (demographically) and doing the same thing (spending most of the day reading books that have nothing to do with anything, and then fooling around with your friends without any supervision for the first time) and doing it on your parents (or the bank's) dime.

So if you are fortunate to have that dime, how about do something that would be much more beneficial: don't go to college. Spend a year learning to paint, or taking singing lessons, or learning yoga in India (getting in shape, meeting people from all over the world, learning Eastern philosophy) or any of 100 other things that will actually better your life, force you to meet new demographics, and do it for much cheaper than the cost of college.

Then, after a year or two of that, why not go to college then – if you still even want to?

SCHOOL

If you were to give one piece of advice to a high school freshman, what would it be?
@williamsjohn

Drop out.

High school is a jungle. Why do you think many high schools have metal detectors at the front door? Places with good, healthy people don't have metal detectors at the front door.

People get hit, they get bullied, they get spit on, they get laughed at. Or maybe this was just me. I easily generalize so call me on it if I'm wrong.

The other day I met a 25 year old on his third business. The other two were successful. The third one just raised a million.

He dropped out of high school. He told me, *"one day I realized I knew how to learn things. I could learn anything I wanted to. So what did I need school for?"*

You can say *"socializing with your peers."* Is that really so great in high school? It wasn't so great for me.

So my advice is: drop out, start businesses, spend time with your friends when they get out of prison every day at 3 pm. And the rest of the time, learn what you want to do and do what you want to do. You might never have that chance again so why waste that in a prison?

How can education be improved? @StealthAviator

I assume he meant education for grades 1-12. I wrote about this recently in "Shakespeare is Awful, Jefferson was a Rapist, and PI is Useless."[1]

My basic assumption is that grades 1-12 are too standardized (higher test results for many schools result in more state funding) and not individualized enough.

For instance, both of my kids love drawing Manga comics. But there's no way for them to do this in school. And after school they are buried in homework and then tired. So whatever skills they developed this summer when they were drawing a lot will start to fade.

1 http://bit.ly/oMh8Ry

The other thing is: most things we learn in grades 1-12 we have to relearn anyway. Or we forget. I asked one friend my age the other day, *"who discovered electricity?" and he answered instantly: "Ben Franklin"* because that is what we were taught in grade school. It happens to be the wrong answer. Anyone hear of William Gilbert in the 1600s?

So here's how I would reform it: since we know grades 1-12 is just glorified babysitting so parents can work, why not hire a bunch of good moms (or dads) to watch over the kids while they play outside, read books, draw, and do whatever they want. Keep them out of harm, and guide them if they ask questions. Also let them play and learn on computers if they want.

And that's it. Will save money, result in smarter kids, result in more active kids (less obesity), and result in more kids finding their passions instead of being killed by standardization.

PUBLIC SPEAKING

I'm a groomsman in a large out of town wedding and was asked to make a roast at the dinner. I hate public speaking. What's your best advice?
@Trader220

I have never given a roast. But I have been asked twice to help someone else write their and prepare for their roast, and it worked out well. I have four pieces of advice:

READ THE POST: "11 Unusual Methods for Being a Public Speaker."[1]

WATCH 30 MINUTES OF STANDUP COMEDY ABOUT A HALF HOUR BEFORE THE ROAST. I had to give a talk for Fidelity last

1 http://bit.ly/jFlvrL

week. The talk was about stocks. Did I prepare by reading the Wall Street Journal? Of course not! I prepared by watching Ellen Degeneres do standup and watching an episode of the Jon Stewart Show. They have perfect timing. To even have 1/10 of that rub off on you will multiply your abilities by ten.

TELL STORIES. Don't tell how you feel. Tell funny stories (but not inappropriate ones) about the groom. Stories have a beginning, middle, and end, and some suspense to them in the middle.

IT'S GREAT THAT YOU ARE NERVOUS ABOUT IT. Don't be afraid to be afraid. Fear is very natural in public speaking. Say to yourself, *"thank god I'm afraid, else I'd definitely give a bad roast."* Observe the fear. Say hello to it. Give it a chair so it can kick back inside of you and relax. Don't try and run from it. It's a natural part of the process of public speaking. When you acknowledge that, then you can get back to the business of being funny for your roast.

BONUS ADVICE: Jeff Ross has written an excellent book about giving roasts. I recommend it.

I'm acing your writing tips (thx!), but could you give us some tips on public speaking, presentations, etc.? @linoxgill

I've given five talks in the past three weeks and I am now preparing to speak at my own radio show. The topics are always changing so I have to do a lot of preparation. I think four of my last talks went well (people laughed at all the jokes) and one was a little flat, but I was able to improve it for a later talk. See: "11 Unusual Methods to be a Better Public Speaker."

Nobody believes me on this but the most unusual method is to "slightly slur your words."

Why does this work? It hypnotizes your body into thinking it's drunk. Then your mind has fewer inhibitions. You get less nervous what people think of you. You say whatever is on your mind.

And usually that's a lot better than saying only the subset of your mind that you think is appropriate.

How to find humor or be funny when doing a presentation?
@PriscillaPWood

The most important thing: be self-deprecating. I have one slide in a presentation, for instance, where right before I turn to it I say, *"The last time I drove a car there was unfortunately a photographer present."* And then I go this slide.[1]

And then people laugh. Come up with a self-deprecating joke every other slide. Talk about bad relationships. People relate to self-deprecation and bad relationships.

Why?

We live in a falsely perfect world. Everyone lies and says they're perfect in some way or other. I see this in the financial space or even the self-help space most of all. But nobody is perfect. Everyone has problems. Everyone has low points. Everyone has failed, has sacrificed, has cried, and has done stupid things. Do be open about yours and people will relate and find it funny. And then love you for giving them permission to fail also.

Ultimately your talk is not about your topic, but about making people feel better about themselves and the world around them. You can also see: "11 Unusual Methods to Be a Great Presenter."[2]

---

1 http://www.jamesaltucher.com/2011/06/11-unusual-methods-for-being-a-great-public-speaker/

2 http://www.jamesaltucher.com/tag/11-unusual-methods-to-be-a-great-presenter/

HAPPINESS

What makes you genuinely happy?
@Nisey7

I try to keep my expectations very low so just about anything will exceed my expectations and make me happy. This can have a double-meaning, one negative and one positive.

The negative is that I seek out shitty things and if they aren't horrible then I'm happy.

The positive is that I try not to constantly seek $100 million dollars, every deal, every girl, and then (since I can't get all of the above) I will be happy.

In general, every day I try to reduce the things that I've spent a lifetime striving for. When these things hit zero, or as close to it as possible (I'm always going to want a roof over my head and a good woman next to me) I know I will be perpetually happy.

Are there important "things" in life that if you care less about them you will be happier? If so, what are those things for you?
@jameskford

Of course! I outline this somewhat in my post "Stop Listening."[1] Try this exercise: Imagine a point when you were a kid when you were happy. At that point, what did you not care about?

- I never cared about the news.

- Or the economy.

- Or gossip news.

1 http://bit.ly/sVdXKo

- Very little about prime time TV (well, "Fantasy Island" on Saturday nights at 10pm I would look forward to).

- I never cared about Europe.

- I never cared about sports (unless I was gambling but then I stopped gambling).

- I certainly never cared about stocks.

Well, one can say, now you have responsibilities. Do I? I do care about my kids. But I still don't need to care about the economy or Europe for the reasons outlined in another question.

I will never care about who is President. Not a single politician has ever made me happier or sadder. So I don't care who is elected ever.

I don't care what people think of me. This sounds harsh. I do, in fact, want people to like my writing. But, if someone is a jerk then I certainly don't care what they think of me. And if someone is a good person and doesn't like me well, then, there's nothing I can do about it. Good thing there's seven billion other people on the planet.

I try to never worry about going broke. When all you do is think of the ways you will go broke, you will go broke. But what I do is I know that if I network as much as possible and come up with good ideas for the people I network with and have the ability to discern who is worthwhile working with and who is not then I know I can always come back from zero. I've done it three times! This is a function of staying healthy in every way.

BEING HONEST

Has revealing so much in your blog and books affected you negatively?
@wrgly

Yes and no. Many people who used to speak to me, no longer speak to me. This includes everyone from friends, to former colleagues, to relatives. Many people have felt I have revealed too much.

In one or two cases, I had to change a story to be less revealing. I'm ok harming myself but never ok if I harm others in what I write.

But overall the blog has been a net positive. I've met MANY new friends. Some people I hope will remain lifelong friends. And I hope that continues. Being honest draws good people to you. Pushes negative people away. I hope the readers of this feel the same way I do.

How do you tell the truth w/o sounding like and a$$?
@socialhotchoco

In my post, "Seven Things Happen to You When You Are Honest"[1] I advocate, obviously, honesty, but not "radical honesty."

Radical honesty is when you have no filter between brain and mouth and is advocated by many as the right way to live. For instance if you want to have sex with your wife's best friend you just blurt that out to both of them. No good!

Most people don't know how to do what I call "constructive honesty."

---

1 http://bit.ly/roqech

I always view honesty as Rule #2, rule #1 being don't hurt anyone. I try to make it a discipline not to even have bad thoughts about someone (very hard for me! Particularly at three in the morning or with random bank tellers.)

I definitely don't want to say something that will hurt someone.

Let's say a friend asks me to look at a blog post. I look at it and don't like it. I will take the time to think about it and then say, *"do X, Y, and Z and this will be a good post."* That's an honest answer, it helps them, and it helps their readers.

Let's say someone asks me about a business idea they have. If I don't like it I will say, *"A lot of things have to happen to make that idea work. I think there;s a few ways you can simplify it to make it easy to do and still valuable to you."*

In other words: put effort into your honesty. Honest without effort is like shitting on the floor in the middle of your house. Nobody will visit you after that, and before long, you won't even like yourself.

What do you think of the phrase "guilty pleasure" and do you have any?
@JenShahade

Before I answer this let me share with you that Jen Shahade is one of my favorite chess players. A former US Women's chess champion and author of two great books, *"Chess Bitch"* and *"Play Like a Girl."* I've read both and benefited just as much from the second as the first.

Now: Guilty Pleasures.

Everything has consequences, good and bad. Everything you do. You can't avoid it. Keep that in mind with this answer.

There's three types of guilty pleasures:

1. Those that hurt others. For instance, cheating on a wife. The consequence is that your pleasure is fleeting. Your sadness is painful (when you are back with your wife and miss the other person), and the consquences could be awful (the pain you cause everyone or even the pain caused by the withholding of love you are giving to your guilty partner).

2. Those that hurt you. For instance, eating that huge chocolate cake at 4 in the morning when nobody else is up. The pleasure is delightful. The consequence is when the cake is gone, and when you go back to sleep and wake up later, feeling ill.

3. Those that give you shame. For instance, a guilty pleasure for me is playing chess online. It doesn't really hurt me. But I feel ashamed that I'm not being more productive.

My goal is to eliminate #1 completely from my life. #2 mostly (but be aware of the consequences) and with #3 it's trickier. I want to turn guilty pleasures into real pleasures.

Where does the shame come from? Some sense of *"I have to be perfect."* Or *"I must never procrastinate with games."* Perfection only leads to shame because the only way to be creative, to be fun, to be flexible in life, to roll with life's punches is to be imperfect.

My goal is imperfection. To thrive in it. To thrive in my guilty pleasures until they transform me into a life of contentment.

How do I make my unknown website popular? @ThePorchHound

It's funny how "honesty" becomes a strong competitive advantage. Your entire competition is dishonest. I'm not saying they are lying. They are just slick, or are hiding the truth in various ways. They might give "10 best ways to find success" but don't talk about all the times they failed.

In 1995 (I forget the exact site) there was a girl who was a narcoleptic. She slept 20 hours a day. But, she had a diary she kept online (what we would call a blog now). And because she so honest and sincere about what she was going through, she had more hits per day than People Magazine's fledgling website.

Sincere voices always rise to the top. Honesty and bleeding are so easy for us to do and yet NONE of our competitors do it. Be honest and you will rise to the top. See: "33 Unusual Ways to Be a Better Writer."

One great example is... Google. Imagine being a consulting company but whenever a client comes to you, you say "no, you should go to my competitor over here."

That's what Google does. If you type in "cancer," Google itself has no content about cancer but will point you to all of its website competitors that do have information that can help you about cancer. Consequently, Google is the most popular website in the world. It's the source. And his is why Yahoo websites are number two. Yahoo is also a source. Become a Source. You do that through honesty, through fearless bleeding, so people know that your site or business first is the truest spot for information that we all need. See: "How Honesty can make You Rich."

Bluffing in business and love. Is it lying? Is it bad, ok, or a necessary evil?
@jhilderley

In life you have 7 billion competitors (the other humans who live here). How do you separate yourself apart? Well, this is easy. 99.99% of them bluff/lie every day.

Cultivate constructive honesty (as opposed to "radical honesty").

Then you will stand out in any beauty contest with the other seven billion people. You will rise up and shine versus your peers. You will rewards you couldn't expect.

GETTING THINGS DONE

How do you stop yourself from wasting time? It has become an addiction which leads to frustration at the end of the day.
@jaideepkhare

I am the biggest time waster of all. I was having breakfast a few weeks ago with Naval Ravikant, the founder of *Angelist*. He refers to the ritual of doing all the Internet checks as "the loop." The loop of checking Twitter, Facebook, emails, blogs, analytics, news, etc.

After that breakfast I timed how long my particular loop took. I thought it would be about three or four minutes. It was eighteen minutes. And that didn't count me responding to anything. And I do that loop about ten times a day. That's 180 minutes. Three hours! Holy...!

So here's what I'm doing. You can't stop cold turkey. That is like a complete alcoholic stopping suddenly and at once. You wake up in the middle of the night with the shakes right away, and if you don't end up in a hospital where they are pumping new blood into you then you can die.

One minute a day I'm taking out one of the things I do to waste time. There's the loop, there's playing extra games of chess online. Etc. One minute a day. By the end of the year I should be down from about 250 minutes a day to about 20 minutes a day. That will be good.

And my three year goal, as I mentioned in "My Minimalism Manifesto"[1] is to get down to 30 minutes of Internet time a day. Maybe I will find other things to fill that time but I hope they are fun, productive things.

---

1 http://bit.ly/rMTIyn

That's it. One minute a day gets rid of. Don't kill yourself trying to do it all at once. You'll get the shakes and die. Just one minute a day.

How do you organize an overwhelming amount of work? How do you make sure you do what you have to do in a day/week?
@flabastida

There are two answers. Just like there are two answers to the question: *"How can I have more money?"*

Answer #1: You make more.

Answer #2: You spend less.

And it's not one or the other. You have to do both.

A "week" has three characters in the story of your life: the events of the week, you, and the energy you start the week with.

Like in any good story, the three characters have problems at the beginning of the story, solve them throughout the story, and hopefully live happily ever after at the end.

So let's see how they can do it:

Character #1: The events of the week. You only have a finite amount of energy. Nobody has infinite. Or we'd be like god or superheroes or something. So assume you have a finite amount of energy. And, to live a wholesome life you need to focus that energy on several things: your family, your friends, the people who love you, your own creative projects, staying healthy, and finally, the projects that advance your career. You also need to find some silence in your life.

So pull out a waiter's pad right now and make the list: what events over the next week cover all of the above areas. You need to cover all of them. If anything is out of balance (your work projects) then reduce it. Now.

I'm not saying your work life isn't important. You'll actually have a more successful work life if you reduce the number of work-related events you have to attend to over the next week. I'll tell you my work schedule:

- When I am in New York City I do no more than one meeting in the morning and one meeting in the afternoon.
- When I write articles for others I try to do no more than one per week.
- When I do a work-related favor ("can you look at this company?") I do no more than one per week
- When I work on my blog I write every day but I post no more than 4-5 times per week.

This is the right balance for me that leaves me time to have silence for myself, spend time with Claudia, spend time with my kids.

What if you have a corporate job? Same thing: Try to do no more than one meeting in the afternoon and one in the morning. Try to spend some time working on your projects. Spend some time networking and/or helping other people with their projects, and make sure you have time for silence.

Character #2: YOU. You need to find time for yourself or you'll never recharge. Too many people have said to me, *"I need to just finish building this business and then I can get back in shape."* SORRY. That doesn't work. You might die before you finish building that business. It's important to consistently do some variation of the Daily Practice I recommend either in this post or in my latest book. I say this not because I'm trying to push you into anything but because I know it worked for me andsince I started recommending it a year ago, I've seen it work for many others.

Here's how it goes, within 1 month you start to have ideas flowing (almost how you would be if all you ate were eggs, fruits, and vegetables – flowing!). Within 3 months you are an idea machine with double the energy. Within six months your life is completely different.

Character #3: Your energy. All I can say is: every six months my life is completely different. And with double the energy. Go for it.

How do you make more hours in the day? @MrJNowlin

Gandhi has a great quote on this. Someone said that with all of his responsibilities he probably should be not be meditating for a whole hour every day. He replied, "I guess I need to meditate for two hours per day."

Time management is a myth. You have the time. You don't even really need to manage it that much. For instance, going through "the Internet loop": email, Facebook, Twitter, news, etc. For most people that takes 15-20 minutes and they do it up to 10 times a day. Do it twice a day.

But if that's hard we must take more extreme measures: No TV, no alcohol, no dinners outside the house (ideally, no dinner past 7 pm or even earlier) and wake up an hour earlier.

And, if you can, no meetings. And if you have a meeting, make it a walking meeting. Walk around the block for your meeting. So you get exercise also and the meeting goes faster. Or don't allow any chairs in the meeting room. I can guarantee the meeting will only be five minutes then.

And don't waste time making excuses about this. Or complaining to me about it. I'm pretty busy also. So I don't watch TV, I don't waste time at dinners outside the house, I wake up an hour earlier, I try (please god give me the strength) not to do the "internet loop" too many times during the day. I don't take on meetings (or, rarely – I pack all my meetings into one day a week and then go from meeting to meeting).

So I've saved time.

Now, my big challenge – what to do with that extra time? So I write a lot. And help businesses I'm involved with. But I want to take even that down a notch. Spend more time with people I love. Spend more time exercising and reading. I hope.

You seem to be a man of lists. Do you have a daily to do check list that you cross things off or is it a more organic process?
@iChmpneGrl

Yes! Here's part of my list.

- I sleep 8-9 hours.

- I read books by writers with strong voices so I hope some of that voice rubs off on me when I begin writing.

- By 6 am I'm writing (I'm on my third cup of coffee by then).

- Around 9 am I start thinking of ideas for making money, writing ideas, book ideas, distribution ideas, helping others ideas, networking ideas.

- Then the day begins. I try to respond to as many people who have written me as possible if I don't have meetings in the way.

- Sometime in afternoon I try to write 1000 words on a novel. If I can do that 2/3 of days then I'll have the equivalent of four novels done within a year. So we'll see if I can stick to this!

- Asleep by 7-8 pm.

I avoid anything that's a time waster: too much social media, I don't read news. No pop culture. No Angry birds or other games. No emails with people who hate me or who I don't like. No prime time TV. No more than two meals a day. No junk food. No gossiping. All of the above taken together saves me about three hours compared with how I used to live my life.

SOCIAL AND GENERAL MEDIA

Twitter or Facebook?
@jennablan

Both. With Twitter I can keep my finger on the world's pulse. With Facebook I can keep my finger on my friends' pulses. Hopefully every day both are alive and healthy.

And with only one of the above companies, it would be hard to track both pulses, both of which are very important to me

Does Twitter make us worse writers or better writers overall? Do you think 140 characters is about right or would you prefer more?
@JenShahade

I like Twitter because there's a "time limit" just as much as a word limit. The time limit forces people to ask you or interact with you in a way that takes no time at all to read and understand and no time at all to respond.

We can then take the time to expand on the answers. So I think Twitter is a wealth of non-stop short ideas and we can pick and choose which ideas become bigger, become the ones that consumer our minds with more words than are probably necessary.

My answer at the time was slightly different but I stand by this also because Twitter is a place where many friendships develop over 140 words:

140 words is a great way to begin a conversation. More than 140 words (via email, say) is a great way to continue a conversation, and face-to-face is a great way to end a conversation, and perhaps begin a real friendship.

I just started a Linkedin ad campaign to jump start my network in a new city, any other good ideas? @bgin2end

I'm not sure a Linkedin campaign works at all to jumpstart a network. I think a little more elbow grease is needed.

The best thing is to, everyday, list 10 people you would like to network with. Come up with 10 ideas for them and send to them for free and say, can I buy you a coffee? This accomplishes the following three things:

1. Shows people you are thinking about their concerns, perhaps more than they are

2. The interaction with you can potentially make them money

3. And it can also get them a free coffee

I think roughly one out of ten will answer depending on who they are and the quality of the ideas. I think it will also grab you a higher caliber of network than a generic ad campaign will (not saying that bgin2end's campaign is generic since I haven't seen it but I think most campaigns are generic in order to hit a wide audience).

You can call this "personalized networking" in that it is like "personalized medicine." Medicine that works based on a person's unique DNA.

FAQ ME

You don't read newspapers so how do you keep up with the news?
@socialhotchoco

Three answers:

1. Who cares about the news? Name one thing in the news today that will make me any happier. Most of the media lies to me to make me panic more. I don't want to panic more. So I won't read the news.

2. When I go on TV I might read a few research reports to get up to speed.

3. Or, I might not. The news never actually changes: Europe, Kim Kardashian, economy worries, everyone's angry, everyone's depressed, election blah blah blah. The news is the same every single day. I know how to respond to the news whether I read it or not. I'd rather read a funny book than read the news. That will make me happier during those twenty minutes. In fact, the best way I prepare for a TV appearance is by watching YouTube clips of Ellen Degeneres doing standup.

Try it, today: instead of reading the news (even the gossip news), read a non-fiction book where you can learn something, or read a funny book where you can laugh at something, or call your kids, or do something where you can actually add to the value of your life instead of decrease from it. Try that every day now for a week.

See the difference?

Some people sleep walk. Others sleep eat or talk in their sleep. I apparently sleep news.
@jaltucher would be disappointed.
@iamtiffani

By the way, this wasn't a question. She just happened to tweet this while I was doing the Twitter Q&A.

Social And General Media

Here's my worst habit when I'm trying to sleep eight hours.

I wake up to go to the bathroom at 2 in the morning. This, in itself, is annoying. I'm dead tired. I'm in the middle of a dream, and suddenly in the dream I have to go to the bathroom. But everywhere I go, there's someone already there. So I have to run around in my dream to find another bathroom. It never ends until I finally wake up at 2 am and go to the bathroom.

I'm so tired, I think to myself: well, at least I'll fall back to sleep right away. I'm too tired.

But then I get back in my bed. I have my iPad, my laptop, my phone, and maybe even some headphones within three feet of me.

I figure, *"I'm so tired, I might as well check what's going on for a few seconds. Its too tempting."*

iPad On: Email, Twitter, Twitter mentions, blog, blog stats, Facebook, S&P futures, Amazon book rank. And god forbid, The News.

And now I'm up. Why did that one person write that one email? Or, why is the world so screwed up? Or... do I need to delete that negative comment right now?

Claudia is sound asleep next to me. Doesn't she even care what's going on in the world at 2 in the morning.Now 3 in the morning? Doesn't' she want to know what my book fell in Amazon ranking? Or that I got an email about that deal I was working on? Has she given up so easily that her eyes are just closed and she's off in her own dreams, flying across her own astral landscapes while I lie here awake, sick, puking in my brain with every pixel in the darkness laughing at me?

Maybe I'll read a book for fifteen minutes. That will make me sleep. I'm up anway. Maybe I can even get work done. So then I read until 4am. I've been up two hours. Normally I would've woken up between 4 and 5 so now I fall back to sleep and I don't wake up until 7 am and I'm totally exhausted now.

This is bad.

So I replied to @iamtiffani. Screen diet. No screen between 6:30 pm and 8 am.

We never had screens before and we lived. Why do we need to see the screen between those hours now? We'll sleep better. Make love better. Eat better. Be less stressed. Less anxious. Less needy (I won't need to check my number of Twitter followers for an entire 13.5 hours a day.)

But it's hard. For people with screen addictions (me), it's very hard. So do this. Try it for five days. Starting today. Just do it. No screen between 6:30 pm and 8 am. That's too hard? Poor baby! Ok, try this: between 7:30 pm and 7 am.

Please, I beg you. Because I'm selfish. Because I know the world will be a better place if we all just try this screen diet.

Let's Occupy Sleep and become in the top 1% of people who live well-rested, less stressful lives. Then we will inherit the Earth.

Why do you always advise to ignore the media, yet regularly contribute to hype and fear monger publications? @robtoole

Every day the headlines get worse and worse and then, when the worst doesn't happen, the media forgets to apologize. Whatever happened to the radiation that was supposed to wash up on the shores of San Francisco from Japan? Everyone got sick taking iodine pills. No radiation. No apology.

And now Greece. What is it with Greece? Since 40BC Greece has never been a self-sufficient country. They were also dependent on funds from others (last: we funded them to keep the Soviets out of the Mediterranean). They never ever had money. Why they were put in the Euro union is beyond me.

And now the media wants us to worry about them even though their effect on our economy is less than 1/10 of 1%. It might even be more like 1/1000 of 1%.

So why do I go on? To try to do my little to set the record straight although it probably accomplishes nothing. I think people at home are so used to hearing doom and gloom all the time I'm hoping that a little bit of optimism will be good for them before we all talk ourselves into a Depression (little "d" or big "D").

What's the best (most responsible/useful) way to keep up-to-date on what's going on in the world? @ryan_a_lane

Do the opposite of what everyone else does: read nothing. Why do I need to keep updated?

I once gave a talk at a major newspaper. Afterwards several of the reporters came up to me and said, *"that was totally different than how we analyze the news. We usually have no idea what to say. Like if the market goes down we say, 'market down due to oil fears.'"* This was in 2004 that I gave this talk. It's gotten a lot worse since then. Now the media tries to find the most crazy thing we can be afraid of and they put that on the cover.

And there's no news source that's different. So today, rather than reading any news at all I finished off a book of short stories I was reading ("Knockemstiff") and started reading Stephen Levy's new book *"In the Plex."* I've been reading Levy since his book *"Hackers."* I also read some poetry by Charles Bukowski. Then I started my day.

Reading any information source for up to date news will only make one stressed, confused, uninformed, and generally in a bad mood. So why bother?

HEALTH

How much of being healthy has to do with being independently wealthy enough to not sweat the small shit? @Andrew_Ferri

A lot and a little. Having money definitely solves your money problems. Which means you don't have to worry about paying the rent. You don't have to worry about going broke. You don't have to work a back breaking or mind breaking job from nine to five. You don't have to be scared.

I really hate being scared. I know it affects my health in every way. So it makes a lot harder for me to live to my potential. No matter what, can you check these four boxes every day?

PHYSICAL – do a little something that improves your health physically, no matter what your personal financial condition is? When I was in India doing yoga a year ago, the main teacher, Sharath Jois, said: "rich? Do your practice. Poor? Do your practice. Problems with your girlfriend? Do your practice. All will come."

EMOTIONAL – what can you do today that will improve your life just slightly on an emotional level? Can you be kind to your fiancée? Can you spend time with a friend? Can you NOT respond to someone who provokes you?

When Atisa, a Bengala meditation master from 1000 AD, brought the 57 lojong slogans to Tibet to transmit Buddhism to the Tibetans he was very nervous they would fall on deaf ears. How come? He had heard the Tibetans were very peaceful and had no worries. And if they had no worries, they would have no challenges to work through in order to become better people.

Well, it turns out he was wrong and Tibetans, like everyone, have much to work through, emotionally, mentally, spiritually, etc.

Health

MENTAL – can you and do you still come up with ideas every day?

SPIRITUAL – can you and do you still think of the people you are grateful for each day? Can you pray for two minutes a day or sit and try to think of nothing.

You can do these four things each day, with or without money. To mis-quote Sharath: do your *Daily Practice*[1] and all things will come.

Do you get a flu shot every year?
@RichP

I haven't had the flu ever since I stopped drinking alcohol

After I fix myself, how do I find others who are also "fixed?
@kjepeneter

The question is really asking: I'm healthy – now I want to meet other people who are healthy. Healthy not just physically but emotionally and in other ways.

The answer is that you don't have to worry: when you are the beacon of light in the gray storm, the other boats that have survived will naturally come to you. This is a law of the universe. Like attracts like is a cliché because it works.

I have "met" better friends through writing than just about through any other means in my life. For me, I wasn't ready to meet good friends until recently. Now I am. And when you are ready, things happen.

What about a girlfriend, does it hold for that also?

Yes it does. The way I was able to meet the love of my life was when I made a conscious decision to be emotionally healthy: not get obsessed over anyone, not try too quickly for sex, not drink alcohol, but find someone who I really liked/loved and thought

1 http://bit.ly/fuiRS9

would be a good partner for the rest of my life. Someone who I could not only kiss but eventually die with.

More seaweed crackers now. I'm obsessed with these things. I can even hear Claudia doing yoga upstairs. But I don't think seaweed is heavy enough for disqualifying me from doing yoga. I'll catch up to her later.

COMING UP WITH IDEAS

What's your technique for coming up with ideas? @JonasNielsen

Let's say you are an excellent archer. You hit the bull's eye every time. But then you stop for five years. You pick up a bow and arrow. Chances are you won't hit the bull's-eye. Your muscles have atrophied. Your skills have gotten weaker.

It's the same thing with the idea muscle. Most people have let their idea muscle atrophy. The key is to start aiming for the target again, whether you miss or hit. But get up early and set up the target and start shooting arrows every day.

Write down ideas every single day. Bad ideas and good ideas. Don't judge them at first. Just brainstorm, even if it's a shitstorm.

Here's my post on nine ways to become more creative. This will help in the long-term with idea generation.

I can guarantee this. Idea generation every day, combined with other aspects of the Daily Practice which I talk about it my last book,[1] *I Was Blind But Now I See*, will change your life completely within six months.

1 http://amzn.to/ppDrlh

BUSINESS IDEAS

In a business, is an idea the most valuable part of the creation?
@greenjobseeker

No!

I'll give you an example: In 2006 I had an offer from a bank to buy the fund of hedge funds I was managing. The offer was a good offer except... they wanted me to sign a six year employment agreement. And if I quit at any point I'd have to give all the money back. Even my lawyer said, *"I thought slavery was outlawed."* So I couldn't take the deal.

So I outlined ten ideas I thought could be good businesses. Nine of those ideas were bad ideas. Anybody can outline ten business ideas. Anybody can outline nine bad ones.

Then I spec-ed out each business, I put the specs on elance.com, I took in over 100 possible bids from developers who wanted to create the businesses, and then I hired one for each idea, including for Stockpickr.com, which worked out well for me.

So the ideas were bullshit. You need to always practice the idea muscle else you won't have any good ideas. But the actual important step was the next step: the spec-ing out of each site, using elance.com to hire a developer, paying the developer to get started, and then starting.

The idea held the ladder. But I had to climb the ladder to change the lightbulb. Climbing the ladder, despite my fear of heights, was the most important part.

If you have an idea that the market isn't ready for, do you sit on it or build it out anyway?
@chrislopez

I had ten ideas and nine were bad. Maybe the market wasn't ready for them. Who knows? I'd be broke now if I had tried to really pursue them instead of quickly cutting my losses.

Since 1990 people have been building apps for wireless devices. I would say the market only started getting ready for those apps in 2010. (I know this, having started a wireless business that the market was not ready for back in 2000).

So, ideas are a dime a dozen. If you have an idea that the market is not ready for, come up with a new idea.

BUSINESS AND ENTREPRE-NEURSHIP

Is it possible to start a business in this worldwide depression?

Groupon started in November 2008! Don't let media fear stop you! Many people were critical of this answer. How come? Because of all the media hype pulling Groupon's numbers apart and saying this is a horrible business.

FACT: Groupon is the fastest growing revenues business in history. They started less than three years ago and have 1.5 billion in revenues this year. The founders have already cashed out probably close to a billion dollars.

Someone said, "But they don't make money."

Excuse me, isn't it enough in less than three years to be pulling down $1.5 billion in revenues? Most companies don't get to, or don't even want to, be profitable until they've been in business 5-10 years. They have to grow first. Amazon took a decade and now they are spewing profits right in our faces and they will continue to do so forever.

November, 2008 was a scary month:

- The financial system was collapsing
- Unemployment hadn't yet skyrocketed but was about to
- I was lying on the floor of countless hotel rooms crying about my lack of luck
- Company after company was going out of business

Did that stop the Groupon guys? Should it stop you, just because they aren't yet profitable? And, by the way, I can find countless examples of companies started in the Great Depression that became amazingly profitable. But let's leave it at this: don't let the news stop you from beginning your path to World Domination.

How do you start a business when you have no money? how do you minimize risk of losing everything @lakergod

In 1994 I had no money and I started working at HBO. When I say I had no money, I had $0. As I've written before I lived in a one room apartment with a guy, Elias Zamora, who made his living gambling chess in Washington Square Park. I slept on the futon, he slept on the couch. I had a garbage bag next to the futon that had all my clothes including a suit I'd pull out each morning to get to work at HBO.

When you work at a big corporate giant you see everything they are doing wrong, all the holes that are missing. You start to think: *"they don't have X. They don't have Y. If they only had Z then their business would be better."* Every day you can come up with 10 things they don't have that would make their business better.

You can build those ten things.

And guess what: you have a ready customer: the company you work for. Or, if not them, then their direct competitors.

That is, at a high level, how I started my first business. I still had a full time salary. But I started making things for them and for other companies that I sold in a freelance capacity. Until it was too big and I was too busy and I was making too much money so I had to quit.

And quitting even then is still a leap of faith that requires courage. But staying at a company for 15 years until you are inbred requires a sad sort of courage as well.

Every day take a little jump. Jump over a puddle. Jump over an alligator crossing the street. Jump over your own fears. Eventually you'll land in the pleasure dome and hopefully you get to stay there.

To summarize: find a customer that will pay you. That minimizes your risk.

Off the top of your head, what would you consider the best 3 entrepreneur books?
@codymort

There are several questions here. What is an entrepreneur? What makes a good book about entrepreneurs? And what are the best books I have read.

An entrepreneur is not a businessman. He's not a billionaire. He's not necessarily a leader. I'm going to change the definition a little bit.

The universe is going in a certain direction. Atoms are in motion; quantum particles are on their endless journey. An entrepreneur is like a god that puts his hand into the universal soup and changes the direction of things so that the resulting worldscape that is created is now different.

An entrepreneur can be a businessman, an artist, an employee, a creator, a mystic.

His mind is pulsating on a different rhythm than everyone else. He is either born this way, or learns it by seeing it in his colleagues, or gets it by clearly seeing the holes and gaps around him that can be filled when everyone else is somehow missing them.

His mind knows how to solve problems when the universe doesn't go the way he has planned. His emotions are free from conflict and from the daggers constantly being thrown at him by the people who are jealous or refuse to believe his new ideas. He is physically fit. He knows how to surrender when defeated and move onto the next event because he had confidence that in the long run things work out for the independent thinkers and souls of the world.

What are the best books for entrepreneurs?

The Rational Optimist, by Matt Ridley. This one book alone shows how we live in a world where not only humans mate and evolve but ideas mate and evolve even faster.

Understanding this one idea and seeing it in action through Ridley's examples will inspire you to dip into that evolutionary pool and inspire yourself.

Wallace Wattles: The Science of Getting Rich. Forget Napoleon Hill. Forget the power of positive thinking. Forget the *"Law of Attraction"* or *"The Secret."* The source of all of these books is a book written in 1900 by a relatively unknown, Wattles.

I Was Blind But Now I See, my book. The purpose of my book is threefold:

1. How society, commercialism, corporate America, and government, are constantly hypnotizing the everyday person to conform to a definition of Happiness and Success that is far removed from reality.

2. How to recognize and reverse that hypnotism.

3. How to start from the core within and get back physical, emotional, mental, and spiritual health so that you can go on to be the creator, inventor, innovator, artist, entrepreneur you were meant to be.

Should one build a prototype or get a venture capitalist first?
@wkarmistead

Absolutely yes, build a prototype first. Go to elance.com or scriptlance.com, put a basic spec of your project up on the site (don't worry about anyone stealing the idea). You will have a reverse auction to see what programmers will do to your project. Pick a programmer (cheap, but look at their recommendations and call references), and build the project for $2-4k (assuming a minimal feature set is cheap enough). Why do this instead of going to a VC first?

- Once you have a site up your value is higher.

- You will learn extremely valuable things in the process of building your site: you will come up with new ideas, learn what obstacles and competition might exist, etc

- You might have a chance to get a paying customer, or users. This also values your company higher.

- You might realize it was a bad idea. Easier to move onto the next idea if it were your own money.

- Why waste time pitching your invisible project when you can use that time to do valuable thinking and building.

- You might never need VC money.

How can I start a business and sell it within two years while making lots of cash?
@jeredbare

I can just say what the easiest method that I used was. I had zero business experience. But I started a service business (making websites for others) and I didn''t leave my job until I had several clients (HBO, most notably), and then you build it until you sell it. Then repeat the process.

If I were going to do things a little differently I'd change two things:

- I would start off as "service" but then productize the service. For instance, in my first successful business I would've changed the "service" to a "product" that made and built websites. Product businesses sell for higher value. I had written all the software that we used again and again to make the backbone of websites but I didn't realize that the smart thing was to productize it.

- Most important: I would've just kept the cash instead of trying to reinvest it in stocks to make more. My biggest regret is making that money and then losing it all that first time and then having to start from scratch again and again.

Is being a tech entrepreneur in the Midwest impossible? Do I have to move to the coast?
@kernicus

I gave a talk last year at a venture capital conference in Des Moines, Iowa sponsored by John Pappajohn, an 83 years "young" entrepreneur himself who I write about here in a post written on my birthday last year (there's a specific reason I wrote it that day).

The room was filled with potential entrepreneurs, each with amazing ideas for tech, energy, marketing, and other sectors.

I absolutely think being on the coasts is the worst way right now to be an entrepreneur. There's a million little startups begging for money from VCs and angels. The problem is there's also a billion little parties, meetups, tech meet-ups, etc. where everyone parties, listens to boring talks, etc. All of this is a distraction.

The Midwest is as cheap as the coasts. Here's what you do:

- Stay in the Midwest so you can live as cheaply as possible.
- Build your product or service.
- Get a customer or traction. Begin to learn what can go wrong in your business.
- Get revenues.

Then decide if you need the coasts or not. Chances are you don't.

I'm a new business owner and we are off to a great start. What is the biggest mistake a new business makes after initial success when looking to expand? *@ajwahls*

DON'T MOVE. Wait until you are so packed you can't fit another single computer and desk in there. Moving spends money, distracts you from your business, and gives you a false feeling of success. Don't move until you are forced.

DON'T HIRE PEOPLE. You don't need an org chart until everyone at the business is working 10 hours a day and working on weekends. Then hire one person. Then repeat. Try to hire people smarter than you. Else, the culture of your business will start to slip.

I feel an overwhelming urge to start a business. I work as a manager at a gym. I respect the owner a lot and he dangles the idea of me owning part of his next gym. Should I view my boss as someone who I can talk to about my desire to be an entrepreneur?
@adampimentel

When I first started my first business I always kept my stable salary from my corporate job going until I had the money, clients, and salary to make the leap.

You want to make a leap. But a leap of faith is too much to ask.

So your instinct seems correct: to hold onto a job you love and are learning from. Whether or not you ask your advice for advice (he won't give you money) is not necessary – he wants to teach you and you want to learn so you will.

On the money side: he will be overbearing as a partner (no judgement against him – thats how people are). So you want to go it your own way or with family or good friends.

I would start thinking in two ways:

Are there any local gyms for sale? You can borrow, beg, plead, and negotiate to pay for it. There are business broker listing sites to see gyms that are for sale.

I'd outline how much it costs to start from scratch a gym: there's renting the space, leasing the equipment (don't buy), insurance, and getting trainers to get clients in there.

Then I'd start brainstorming on how to make your gym special. What does it? Maybe you have post-workout massage in the back so the muscles that are worked on get properly stretched out afterwards (I am making that up – I have no idea about what happens to muscles). Maybe you sell protein powders and you set up "Super Gyms" for people who really want to go for it.

You have the desire. That's great. I had the desire for about 2 years before I was able to make the full plunge although I was making double income for a while (stable and unstable/startup incomes) before I made the leap. I was very cautious.

So:

- Keep the desire.
- Learn everything you can.
- Come up with 10 ideas a day on your business, starting tomorrow.
- Be as cautious as possible.
- Plan the leap, but don't rely on faith. Plan EVERYTHING.
- No partners that you'll hate later. My first partner was my sister. It was a very successful business. but we don't speak. That's what happens.

Quitting my enterprise consulting job after 7 years & starting my own company (technology services based). Any advice? @RobbieAb

Three things:

1. Pat yourself on the back for quitting your job. Quitting is not for everyone. But when you do it, and you do it for the right reasons, it can lead to an enormous feeling of freedom. Here you can read: 10 Reasons You Should Quit Your Job.[1]
2. Now is the beginning of the rest of your life. I used to write for AOL's DailyFinance site. When all of the great employees of that site got laid off I felt really bad for them and wanted to

1 http://www.jamesaltucher.com/2011/05/10-more-reasons-you-need-to-quit-your-job-right-now/

help. I wrote this post, which is good on any occasion where yesterday was the last day of your job: 10 Things to Do if You Were Fired Yesterday.[1]

3. Since you are going off to start your own consulting business I also recommend: The Easiest Way to Succeed as an Entrepreneur.[2]

Build startup on the side slowly, or quit day job get funding and move faster?
@MrJNowlin

Do not leave the day job. By the time I left my day job I was totally able to duplicate my income with my startup. I did not suffer one decrease. I had about 10 clients, including my day job, and I was able to juggle the startup with the day job by giving up on social life. I hired all my friends at either my day job or my startup.

From beginning of the startup until the time I left my job was about 1.5 years. Give it time. I feel like the world is in a startup frenzy right now. Relax. Corporate America as has been traditionally is now officially dead. There's no safety there. There's only hustling now. Always have ideas and you'll eventually be able to leave the day job.

What are your thoughts on employee recognition (entrepreneurial or not) for a company of ~190 employees? Gift cards, recognition in a newsletter, a lunch for over-achieving employees?
@andrealynn

If you have a program of sales incentives already in place ($100,000 in a month gets a trip to Caribbean, etc) then that's fine. Else, I would not do something like that after the fact because some people might feel bad.

---

1 http://www.jamesaltucher.com/2011/03/10-things-you-need-to-do-if-you-were-fired-yesterday/

2 http://www.jamesaltucher.com/2011/04/the-easiest-way-to-succeed-as-an-entrepreneur/

Instead, you want the employees (and really all of the employees) to always feel like there are opportunities to advance in your organization (as opposed to prizes).

Advancement means (depending on how you execute on this) more learning, more money, more opportunities for wealth in the future.

I would sit down with the best employees and ask them specifically what they see their future as. Maybe they eventually want to be entrepreneurs and go out on their own (and that's fine also!), maybe they want a new title, maybe they want to go with you on business development meetings (as long as it doesn't affect their sales meetings), maybe they want a day off to do charity.

But if they know that you personally care about their personal advancement then they will make you the most money and continue to kill for you. I would also ask them if they know anyone like them that you can hire (and then you get rid of the underperformers). This might also make the best employees feel more like managers. Another possibility is stock options for the best of them. This can be done by putting together a stock option program for everyone but that they earn into it based on past and future sales. (i.e. don't give out all the options at once).

Who will be the next Steve Jobs?
@bgin2end

Probably the article I've gotten the most negative criticism on is "10 Unusual Things I Did Not Know About Steve Jobs."[1] When it was on the front page of the Huffington Post all of the kind commenters there were convinced I was a blind idiot and a horrible writer. How could I admire a man as terrible as Steve Jobs? They wondered.

Every day we artists use the tools that flew out of his head onto the planet. Every day our kids watch the shows his persistence

1 http://www.jamesaltucher.com/2011/02/10-unusual-things-i-didnt-know-about-steve-jobs/

in Pixar allowed creators to develop. Every day students use the computers he conceived of starting in 1977. But now he's dead. Is there another one?

Of course there is. There are many. Google, for instance, right now is wiring up Kansas City, Missouri to have 2 GB/sec super-wi-fi. That means you can download an entire movie in 2 seconds. Or the last season of Glee (every show) in about 20 seconds. Larry Page and Sergey Brin have a thirty year vision of what the world will look like: there will be Internet everywhere and blindingly fast, there will be cars driving without drivers, all information will be catalogued and at our fingertips or already in our brains.

Mark Zuckerberg will catalog all of our social interactions, making it easier to effortlessly stay in close contact with our friends no matter how apart in space and time. Every day there are more Steve Jobs' being created, growing up, innovating. He created the mold – but the mold is being filled over and over again. See: "Why are Larry Page and I so Different?"[1]

WEALTH

What's more sane, an abundance or a scarcity mentality? I give money away because I think there'll be more – but I'm not rich. Am I crazy?
@lindsaycampbell

You are the opposite of insane.

After going broke and making it back several times I feel scarred. I have a scarcity complex. It doesn't matter how much money I have, I always feel like I'm broke. I feel like I have to hoard. I feel like the money can go away in a second through either mistakes

1 http://www.jamesaltucher.com/2011/03/why-are-larry-page-and-i-so-different/

of my own, mistakes of the universe, or some magical force stealing from me.

But for me to take money, I have to take careful planned risks. I have to overcome my scarcity complex every day and realize that I deserve money. I work hard, I plan for my risks, I try to check every box, I have to trick myself into not thinking the money is automatically gone, that it's being put to work in engines that will generate more money for me.

A rule of the universe that I've written about is: Give and You Will Receive.[1] Every day try to think of all the ways you can give.

Having an abundance mentality, combined with a healthy risk aversion, is the best way to ultimately receive.

INVESTING

Where does one begin is he/she wants to start investing? @Nisey7

First off, day trading is dead. You can read my "8 reasons not to daytrade"[2] or my "10 Reasons Not to Own Stocks."[3]

That said, I do not think investing is dead.

Read "The Essays of Warren Buffett" by Lawrence Cunningham to see what the master has said over the past 50 years. Note, I'm not even pushing my own book, "Trade Like Warren Buffett." Cunningham's book, compiled from Buffett's letters to investors, is better.

---

1 http://www.jamesaltucher.com/2010/11/give-and-you-will-receive/

2 http://bit.ly/ho28VG

3 http://www.jamesaltucher.com/2011/04/10-reasons-you-should-never-own-stocks-again/

Second, read "The Rational Optimist" by Matt Ridley.[1] Ridley is one of the smartest men alive right now. His book will teach you how to question the assumptions constantly posed and feared by the media and used to scare you. He goes over everything from peak oil, to overpopulation, to wars and violence, and analyzes all the statistics. Why is this useful? How will this help you pick stocks?

It's because picking stocks is not the hard part in investing. Warren Buffett says it succinctly, *"if you have good reason to believe a company will still be here 20 years from now, it will probably be a good investment."* We know Apple will still be here, for instance, so that's a good stock to pick.

The problem is: what do you do the next time there's a 2008 (or even a summer 2011) and all stocks crash. You have to be able to really analyze and say *"is the world ending" or "is this just a blip."*

Look at this chart here of the Dow for instance. Can you see where the crash of 1987 occurred? It's barely noticeable. And in your consciousness even it has to be barely noticeable. That's the hard part in investing. "The rational optimist" plus being healthy and secure in other parts of your life, will help you become a better investor.

The times when I lost the most money investing was not because I was picking bad stocks. Most of the stocks eventually hit new highs long after I sold them. It was because I was either unhappy with my work life or marriage or family or whatever. And so not thinking straight caused me to not invest straight. That's the key to successful investing.

In "Margin Call" there's a quote: There are 3 ways to make a living: be first, be smarter, or cheat. What do you think? @Candriawan

None of those are the answer. There were many search engines before Google, for instance and many social networks before

1 http://www.amazon.com/gp/product/0061452068

Facebook. So they were first but didn't make a living. They all failed. And being smarter doesn't always work either. Microsoft products were never considered best (Steve Jobs gave some funny quotes to Walter Isaacson about this) but they won.

And cheating might work, but also might make you end up worse than you ever were. So all of the methods above could work but they also might fail horribly.

The absolute best, surefire way to make a good living is to help someone else make a good living. If your business or service helps others make money, particularly if your method is scalable, then the amount of money you can make is incalculable.

For instance, when I really needed to make some money, I advised someone on how they can sell their business. They made $41.5 million dollars. I can guarantee you I made good money when that happened. I was spending a lot of time, for free, before that happened. But once he made money, I made money.

Is being "risk adverse" a pathological character flaw? @noahlz

The total opposite! Let's say you hire someone who loves every kind of risk. He smokes crack and screws hookers on the weekends. He power skis on his days off. He gambles all his money in Las Vegas on his vacations.

How long will this employee last? How long will he even be alive? Not very long.

I've been involved in startups for the past 17 years or so. The best startups had every risk planned and accounted for before the business even started. The best entrepreneurs avoid risk, are scared of it, plan for it. Nobody wants risks. They want easy money. The way to get easy money is to have the most noble character trait of all: being risk averse.

It's more risky to stay at the standard corporate job, living out your life afraid of your boss, your mortgage, the economy, stocks, your 401k, and all the other things you are scared of. I hate being scared.

VC companies say "idea's worth nothing, execution is worth everything," do you agree with that? @kortessIgor

I'm going to break it into two parts: What's good for you and what's good for VCs. Both are important.

What's good for you is to get the idea muscle flowing. Everyone says *"ideas are a dime a dozen."* This is true. But 99.99% of those ideas are bad ideas. The idea muscle atrophies within days and most people don't exercise it.

Get a pad today (I use waiter pads) and start writing down ideas. Pick any topic: ideas for businesses, ideas for how your neighbor can get more customers, ideas for novels, etc. It doesn't matter. Cross out obviously bad ideas. Stretch your brain (it hurts, it's like a yoga stretch) to come up with 10 ideas. Okay, now come up with 10 more. Hurt yourself.

Now, are these ideas doable? Cross off the ones that don't have a concrete next step. Fill up the idea list to replace those you crossed off. Now, do you believe you can do these ideas? Cross off the ones you can't or the ones you are not interested in. Replace those on the idea list. Your brain should be sweating by the time you are done.

Note: you just wrote down ten bad ideas. Do this every day. Within six months (assuming the other three areas of your life are healthy) you'll be an idea machine. Don't worry about that yet.

Now: Execution! You just came up with ideas that have a concrete next step. So we know you can execute (again, as long as health is ruling you).

But here's what VCs really care about: *"what have you learned so far?"*

In order to learn from your execution you need traction. You can't just have a product (the first steps of execution) or a service but no traction. You need customers, users, and a learning curve that includes at least one or two mistakes you've learned from along the way. VCs want to hear what you've learned and how the business changed because of those experiences.

Then that shows you have traction, which meant you executed, which meant you developed an idea that they might be willing to fund.

NEGOTIATION

Is there such thing as good, honest and fair negotiator? @socialhotchoco

A very good negotiator once told me, *"In a good negotiation, all sides walk away happy."* Everyone gets what they want.

If this doesn't happen, then the results of the negotiation will have negative consequences down the road. Maybe people won't work as hard because they feel they got the short end of the stick. Maybe lawsuits will develop, etc.

[See, "The 3 Secrets of Negotiation"[1]]

1 http://bit.ly/sndKHq

Is it better to settle with someone with no integrity that wronged you in a business dispute and pay x or fight it and potentially pay 5x in fees?
@ajwahls

Always: Settle, forgive, forget, move on. Life is short. We're a tiny dot in the Universe. Our lifespans on this tiny dot are even tinier. Your interaction with this hateful person is even tinier. Don't make it bigger than it needs to be in your short life on this tiny planet.

Settle, and move on and get rich and happy. What could be a better answer than that?

TRADING

What advice would you give to someone like me who wants to trade for a living but can't seem to get over fear of losing?
@MzAprilShowers

Anyone who is interested in trading has several features in common most of the time:

- Intelligent enough to do heavy research on companies or trading systems. I think 99% of traders realize they need to create an edge for themselves and this involves hard work

- An ability to gamble

- They don't want to work for anyone else

These are similar (or the same) as features required by an entrepreneur. I think, ultimately, daytrading is a loser's game [See,

"8 reasons not to daytrade."[1]] and you can use those same attributes to be an entrepreneur [See, "100 Ways to a be a better entrepreneur."[2]]

Am I a fool for continuing to invest in the stock market? I'm self-employed and don't know how to build a nest egg these days.
@teashopgirl

You are not a fool at all although I would stay away from the stock market. I'm bullish on the market and the US economy. But I think too many people without experience buy at the top and sell at the bottom and I also think there are only two types of people who make money in the market:

- People with large stakes who hold forever (Buffett and Gates come to mind)

- People are wired right into the exchanges and make millions of trades a day.

Everyone in the middle gets slashed up and loses money.

I happen to own the children's book Tea Shop Girl (the questioner) has written. When you own stocks you get too distracted to write, particularly during downturns. It's also very hard (Maybe impossible) to write a bestselling fiction book.

But, for someone already in the business, it's possible to write series of books that get consistent (but small advances) that could then produce steady streams of royalty. My advice after more back and forth was to be prolific (Isaac Asimov, for instance, wrote 467 books) and write a 100 books in a series of children books.

1 http://bit.ly/ho28VG
2 http://bit.ly/edLg2J

What's the next bubble?
@Unpacktherat

This might be the wrong question. I don't think there will be any next bubbles. Bubbles imply that an asset class goes up today simply because it went up yesterday (so more and more people flock into it for no reason).

But, the next asset classes to experience enormous returns: biotech and energy.

Biotech because we have 70 million baby boomers retiring. And they are all going to get sick and die horrible deaths. All of them. So whatever we can do to alleviate their pain and extend their lives we will do. There will be pressure on the FDA to relax their standards so drugs can get out the door. And more and more smallcapbiotechs will find a new lease on life as their drugs are used to extend the lives of the retiring baby boomers.

Energy because it's getting cheaper to drill for oil (in the US) using the technology called fracking, which gets oil that was previously hard and expensive to get. This will transform the US into a new Saudi Arabia and reduce our dependence on middle eastern oil.

Of course, I also think social media will do well: whatever the next Zynga, etc. might be.

AMZN or AAPL?
@ChicagoYak

Warren Buffett says that if a company is still going to be here 20 years from now then it is probably a good investment (this isn't always true: Kodak, for instance, GM. Bethlehem Steel, etc).

But clearly Apple is going to continue to innovate. Steve Jobs might be dead but the actual designer of the iPod, iPhone, iPad is

Johnny Ive who is very much alive and 44 years also. [See, "Why AAPL will be the first trillion dollar company"[1]]

And while bookstores are going out of business left and right, Amazon is continuing to thrive and continuing to innovate in industries they were never in before (which reminds me of Apple). I think one can put money in both these companies and never look at them again. The "never looking at them again" is the key to investment success.

What do you think is the outlook for the US market in the next six months? *@artling*

I can answer with a question: Why would the US market go down?. Companies like Apple, Microsoft, Exxon, and Intel, all trade for less than 10 times forward earnings (historical average is 15 times earnings) and they are all growing (Apple has grown 124% year over year), and they all have enormous cash.

Let's look at all the leading indicators that suggest the economy will be good 1 – 6 months from now:

- Rail traffic: up
- Hotel occupancy: up
- Retail sales up: 4% year over year
- ISM manufacturing above 50, saying the economy is still expanding
- Unemployment claims at lowest level since May 2008
- Existing home sales up 18% year over year while housing starts at a low (i.e. demand is up but supply is down so housing prices should go up)

1 http://bit.ly/gXYbfk

I can go on and on. And the stock market is not necessarily related to the economy on a daily basis but I do think the worst is behind us. And the market is in bear market territory (or has been) so now we should get a strong bull market move and then we have an election year which should be good.

Also, when Zynga, Facebook, etc start going public that should be strong for the market. And finally, when banks start lending the $1.6 trillion they have in reserves (and commercial lending is already back full force) then that should be good as well.

So basically: I think the US market is going to go straight up.

THE ECONOMY

What makes you so optimistic about the economy?
@billtheimpaler

There are really two answers to this: personal and public. The personal side is "why should you and I be optimistic right now about finding opportunity?"

Right now, with everyone so pessimistic, is the best time to be optimistic. There's $1.6 trillion extra dollars lying around in the banks. Corporate America has an extra $2 trillion and there's untold trillions in pension funds, retirement accounts, etc that are completely in cash. All of that money will eventually hit the economy. Any business started now that is halfway good will get their hands on that money.

"Getting that money" is the equivalent of *"the Olympics."*

You can't just hold your hand out and get an Olympic gold medal. You have to get in shape. You have to start coming up with ideas. You have to get rid of the crappy people in your life. You have to plan your exit from your corporate job which sucks 10 hours of life (and 50% of your money via taxes) out of you each day. You have to have gratitude for your health and for the loving people around you.

Then you have to start coming up with ideas. What do 76 million retiring baby boomers need? What do 750 million people on Facebook need? What do hundreds of thousands of returning veterans need? And so on. Find the demographic trend, any of them, and feed it. You will get paid for that.

But on a more public level: what makes me an optimist?

- Rail traffic is up! What does this mean? It means people are shipping commodities all over the country. Steel, oil, food, etc. Which means companies are about to start building things, which means companies are seeing demand pick up so they are getting ready to restock inventories, which are at lows. This indicator is almost never talked about in the media outlets. All they talk about is a beach resort in Europe called Greece which has nothing to do with us.

- Hotel occupancy is up. What does this mean? It means business people are traveling again. They are traveling because they are selling something. They don't travel to sell without companies asking for those sales, putting out proposal requests, etc. Things are moving.

- Look at the statistics for Fedex.com (using a site like Compete.com). It's up. It slipped a little when manufacturing dropped 15% in the summer in Japan because of the Earthquake but now it's back up. This means things are being shipped. Goods are being sold. This doesn't mean the economic statistics will be good for last quarter. It means it will be good for next quarter.

- Housing starts up huge. Huge. The biggest since 2006. That means people will get hired again to build houses. That's a huge part of our economy.

- Earnings are killing it. Intel is the bellwether for all technology. Technology has driven the market (for better or for worse) for fifteen years. Intel is killing it. This means people are buying computers and phones. Which means businesses are expanding. AAPL, one of the fastest growing companies, trades for just 8 times forward earnings and has $116 billion cash in the banks. These companies aren't going bankrupt and demand is not going down for their products.

And let's forget all about the basic economic statistics. Google is making cars that drive around on highways without drivers. MIT scientists are working on quantum computers. Every day there's more evidence on how to diagnose and cure various cancers.

We are a smart country, filled with innovators, and nobody comes even close. Sure, maybe China will get close to us by 2050 but that just means they will become our customers instead of just some random country selling us cheap goods.

Don't be a pessimist and hold a sign up and get angry. The time for opportunity is here. Start planning for it.

You can say, *"Well, what about the Eurozone?"*

Let me tell you something about Greece: Greece has only survived by the grace of its good friends since 40 BC. Julius Caesar supported it, other countries supported it, all the way through Ronald Reagan who supported it because of his terror of the Soviet Union. Since then, the Eurozone has supported it. So everyone since 40 BC has known that Greece is what it is: a beach resort on the Mediterranean. Nothing more, nothing less. They won't make the next Google. And maybe they'll pay down their debt, maybe not. And then China will support it. Who knows? But their issues, which have been known for 2000 years, will not bother us one bit.

If shit really hits the fan, what do you think is a good country for a young American to move to?
@M-Knopf

I have a scarcity complex. When I sold my first company it was 1998. I woke up one morning at about 4 am in a panic. In about 28 years I was going to go broke, I thought to myself. And that's after I would make sure my parents and kids had millions of dollars. I got out of bed and walked all over the city. I think I circled the entire downtown Manhattan within about two hours. Just pacing and adding up numbers and always coming up short. 28 years, 30 years if I cut this corner, 27 years though if I fall down this alley.

Downtown Manhattan became a map of my scarcity, my feelings that I was never good enough to make money, that I would never be good enough to hold onto it, that I didn't deserve it in the first place, that eventually I would lose it all.

And guess what? I lost it all. Every single dime. Again and again, since I'm always good at coming up with more ideas. But for me, that feeling of scarcity is the hardest thing to deal with. Why do I have it? I don't know the answer even now.

But let me tell you: nothing is hitting any fan. As Pinker shows, there is less violence in the world now than ever before. Heck, we have toilets, we have literacy, we have the iPad.

Are there people suffering? Yes. And our goal is to make the world better and help them. We can all do that by people the best people we can be first. As I've written before, "Occupy Yourself" first.[1]

Don't' spend your day worrying about whether some bank in Europe is going to default to another bank in Europe. Let's not forget in 1981 that almost the entire continent of South America defaulted. What happened after that? A 2 decade boom in the American economy plus the widespread acceptance and rollout of the Internet, which changes people's lives every day.

1 http://bit.ly/snVZZr

Is there contemptuous behavior in the banks? In government (insider trading rampantly abused by members of Congress where it is surprisingly legal).In all the alphabet city of agencies in between the banking world and the government? In the lobbyists? In the candidates? Of course! But Occupy Yourself first.

Don't run scared to another country. They aren't better. They are, for the most part, far worse. When Havel became leader of the Czech Republic in the "velvet revolution" I was inspired by his first official talk where he suggested change comes from within. He was right, but it still didn't necessarily mean people would listen to him or that the Czech Republic would flourish under his rule.

Focus on every day improving the energy you emanate out to the rest of the world. Then you can live anywhere and be happy and successful and a beacon to others.

What are your thoughts on Greece? @jamesketchell

AAAARGH! Greece! I am so sick of this country already. We first even heard of Greece in May 2010. There were some rumblings. They couldn't pay their debt and everyone wanted to retire by some early age – what? 24 years old they wanted to retire. And then hang out on the beach and get paid by the government.

Then suddenly everyone in the media became experts on the word "contagion." Somehow these beach-goers were going to spread their vile debt contagion throughout the rest of Europe, then the US, then China and Asia and the entire world would collapse. "But James", anchors would say to me on TV, *"can't you see how Greece could create a domino effect"* Blah blahblah. One more blah: Blah!

Let me tell you some fun facts about Greece:

- It's 0.15% of the world's population.

- If you go to Greece (or, in my case, if you go to a pool hall in Astoria, NY which is almost entirely populated by Greek people, and many of the waitresses at the Greek diners were too beautiful for me despite the fact that I wrote my phone number down on $2 bills that I gave out as tips) they have three types of backgammon that they play as opposed to our one. No wonder they want to retire so early!

- The Greek debt divided by the Eurozone GDP is similar to Rhode Island's debt divided by the US GDP. If Rhode Island defaulted I wouldn't care either. Rhode Island, also btw, is a beach resort. Just like Greece.

- Most important: Since the time of Augustus in 20 BC, Greece's bills have been paid by other countries. All the way up to Ronald Reagan in 1989 who was terrified the Soviet Union would have access to the Mediterranean so kept paying Greece's bills. So the EU knew this going into the situation that Greece cannot live without the kindness of strangers. This has been known for 2030 years!

- In 1981, the top 5 banks in the US were 263% exposed to South American countries that totally defaulted! Zero! Thank god the word "contagion" had not been invented yet by some media Einstein. What happened next in the US? 20 year Stock market boom!

So okay, what's our exposure to not only Greece but let's throw in Portugal, Spain, Ireland, and Italy. Other than Ireland, all prior leaders of the world. Total exposure in the top 5 US banks? 8% Glory Be! You know what this means? It means I should never be able to turn on the TV and hear the word "Greece" unless I am watching some backgammon tournament on ESPN 3.

I know you don't think Greece is a big deal, but what about Italy? Big deal, maybe or nothing? @wesbroxson

You're right. Greece, with 0.15% of the world's population, and a similar affect on the EU GDP as Rhode Island has on the US GDP, doesn't concern me at all.

Italy is of course bigger, and one of the largest borrowers in the world. But let's not forget, the headlines were all panicky about Greece. So now they are all panicky about Italy. So you have to take headlines with a grain of salt and let's look at the reality:

Italy managed to borrow $150 billion the other day at much lower yields than people had predicted.

I looked down the list of the largest banks that lent Italy money and I did not see ANY US banks on that list.

Italy, unlike Greece, is made up of people who are increasing their savings rather than decreasing it. So the money is there and now it's up to the government to get them to spend it (as opposed to putting in austerity measures).

Mario Monti, an economist, will be the new Prime Minister and provide a much needed injection of confidence than the scandal-prone Berlusconi

Let's not forget, NOBODY in Europe has actually defaulted yet. And our top 5 banks have only 8% exposure to all the P.I.G.S. countries.

Compare this with 1981: Almost the entire continent of South America defaulted. And our top banks were 263% (!) exposed to their debt. What happened? We went on a 20 year stock market boom.

So I don't read the news. I don't panic. I ignore the headlines. Italy is a nice place to eat dinner and sight see but I'm not going to ever think again about their debt.

Do you still believe the Dow might be up 8,000 points or more in the next several years? @redwings924

I'm an optimist on America. Whenever things seem like they are roughest, the market mistress has a way of doing her dance to confound all of her greatest lovers.

Right now we have:

- $1.6 trillion in the banks.
- $2 trillion in cash in the non-banks.
- Another $3 trillion or so in pension funds and savings accounts.
- Railway traffic is up.
- Hotel occupancy is up.
- Corporate earnings are up.
- Fedex.com website stats are up.
- Inventories are low.
- Existing home sales are up with new home starts down (supply vs demand will create an imbalance eventually).
- Very few IPOs.
- Large numbers of stock buybacks, the greatest in history (again, supply and demand. More shares being removed from supply).

The Economy

All the conditions are set for not only a boom but a bubble. Are bubbles bad? Not for me to judge. But It's good to be on the right side of one if you can get there. Is America doomed ultimately? Who knows. We may have massive problems in the next few years as we continue to transform and suffer through the continued nursery school education of our leaders (both Democrat and Republican). And we may suffer through massive inflation. But the best hedge is buying the stocks that are continuing to innovate and do well. Or starting your own company (which is ultimately the best way to ride a rising stock market, rather than buying stocks that are largely manipulated by unseen power-players).

Do you have any post on this topic:Bubbles, and how its different than the 1st dot-com?
@eycsound

Definitely not. This is the dream of Internet 1.0 come true. What was that dream? That everything would be available, all the time online, cheaper, and we can communicate with anyone we wanted around the world, and of course, we could have more sex with more people than we could have thought possible.

What's the proof?

These are not BS companies. Say what you want about Groupon, it is the fastest growing company (in revenues) in history. Say what you want about Zynga it is the fastest growing company (in profits) in history. Say what you want about the "old" dot-com companies: AMZN, EBAY, and lets throw GOOG (which came a little late to the game) and AAPL, they are all near all-time highs in value, revenues, and profits (which sort of suggests that even Internet 1.0 wasn't a bubble, it was more of a way for the public to play VC. In the VC model there will be zeros and home runs. The public wasn't used to this, so labeled it a "bust" which it wasn't really given the number of companies from then that are at all-time highs now, 1000s% higher).

Internet companies deliver value, help the lives of consumers, and make enterprises get their own jobs done cheaper (the true cause for 9% unemployment is that the Internet created dead weight, just like the invention of machinery for agriculture ultimately ended slavery (not to compare slavery for dead weight but the only reason the south was so intent on "keeping" them was because they had no alternative of getting their fields tilled, harvested, planted, seeded, whatever).

Each generation of the Internet will eliminate deeper levels of corporate slavery. Its our duty:

- To not wonder about boom or bust but take advantage of all the new technologies at our disposal.

- Constantly seek to learn what they are (I am woefully behind. Already turning into an old man in my young age).

- To free ourselves from the boundaries we thought possible.

Long live Internet 2.0

How do you think in this bleak environ small financial services companies will survive? Or how can they? @thefridayguy

So, he really asked a slightly different question but I'm broadening it. Let me tell you the truth: in any sector, in any economy, in any political environment, your only competition is yourself. 99.9999% of the people out there are unhealthy (i.e. they don't exercise their physical, emotional, mental, and spiritual bodies as per "the Daily Practice"). So they are not your competition. You just have to make sure the luck flows your way and it does if you keep healthy on all four of those legs of the chair this world sits on.

Don't forget: Groupon, the fastest growing revenues company in history started in November, 2008, the worst financial month in history since the Great Depression.

I never think about the economy. There's 5 trillion in unspent cash marinating all over the economy, doing nothing, because people are afraid.

Your job is to be healthy and help make them unafraid. To spend that 5 trillion in cash.On you.

NETWORKING

I am in a wedding with a lot of high level executives. Should I network?
@YoavEzer

Yes. I get invited to the occasional dinner where there are a lot of people I would like to network with [See, "Someone wanted to throw a grenade at me"[1]].

The best way to network with someone cold (i.e. you don't know them and know nobody in common) is to give them ideas that can help them make money. If you know who will be at the wedding, research their businesses, come up with 10 ideas for each person how they can improve their business.

It's not like you are going to go up to them and say, *"here are 10 ideas for your business."* But now if you are sitting next to them or find yourself casually talking to any of the people you want to network with, you are ready to instantly go into network-mode if the conversation starts to veer in the direction of their business.

Practicing this ability will get you better and better at it until you no longer have to come up with the lists in advance. You'll be an idea machine at any event, able to manage the balance between casual conversation and idea generation with ease, and everyone

1 http://bit.ly/odzxqm

will say, *"we should have a meeting/coffee/lunch about this over the next week!"*

How to approach and connect with the #1 top notch people if you're young and ambitious?
@joTorsvik

This has happened to me on several occasions. It happened to me when I wanted to get my first real job. It happened to me when I launched my first business. It happened to me when I transitioned my career 360 degrees (twice) and on a daily basis it happens to me.

There is a few things you need to keep in mind, for example:

Develop ideas and give them away for free to the top people in your field. 1 out of 10 will respond. Not because the other 9 are bad people but the ideas might not work for them or they might just be busy. OR, the ideas might be bad. So you have to keep practicing the idea muscle and keep sending out the ideas. Why for free? Because you have to give in order to receive.[1]

For more: 9 Ways To Become a Super-Connector.[2] These ideas work no matter how young you are.

Here are the nine ways I wrote about:

1. INTRODUCE TWO OTHER CONNECTORS – this is an unbelievable technique. If you can introduce two people who are themselves great connectors then you become a meta-connector. They will meet and get along (connectors get along with each other for two reasons: THEY ARE NATURALLY FRIENDLY PEOPLE (hence their ability to connect so easily with people) AND THEY HAVE A LOT OF FRIENDS IN COMMON almost by definition.) If you are in the middle of that connection then they will always remember you and you'll always

1 http://www.jamesaltucher.com/2010/11/give-and-you-will-receive/
2 http://www.jamesaltucher.com/2011/10/the-9-skills-needed-to-become-a-super-connector/

be on their mind for future potential connections they can make that would be useful *for you.* And their rolodexes are immense. So if you need to meet Prince William of England, for instance, or Ellen Degeneres then just connect two connectors and the next thing you know you'll be dancing right down the aisle with Ellen on her show or bowing to Kate Middleton, or whatever you want to do. Ellen? Kate? Uma?

2. INTRODUCE TWO PEOPLE WITH AN IDEA IN MIND: Marsha, meet Cindy. Cindy, meet Marsha. Marsha, you are the best book editor in the world. Cindy, your book is the best book idea I have ever heard. You both can make money together. No need to "cc" me.

   In other words, if you can help two other people make money then eventually, good things will happen to you. In cases where I've been able to do this (rare, but it's happened) I always tell people who say *"what can I do for you"* that *"if they ever find me in the gutter with blood leaking from my mouth and a needle sticking out of the veins in my elbow then at the very least pull the needle out."* That's all I ask. The first time I ever did this I went home (1994) and told my girlfriend, *"I just helped two people make money for the first time ever."* And she said, *"yeah, but what did you get?"* I got nothing. But I felt something. I felt like I had done good in the world and that if I kept doing it, eventually it would return to me. And it did. With those very two people that first time but years later.

3. HAVE A DINNER OF INTERESTING PEOPLE: I've only done this twice. When the last Star Wars prequel came out I invited people from every aspect of my life (friends, hedge funds, writers) to a dinner, I got everyone movie tickets, and it was a fun night. I solidified my relationships with some of my investors, plus some of the funds I was invested in, and I managed to connect people up who later did business together. On another occasion I threw a party for everyone who had been fired by thestreet.com. It got a little awkward when the guy who had done most of the firing (who had himself been fired

right before then) was also there but it was all in good fun. Not sure how much goodwill it created for me. Too early to tell.

But, I much more enjoy *going* to the dinner that I'm invited to. I've met a lot of interesting people. My main problem is that my normal bedtime is about 8 p.m. So sometimes I fall asleep at the table and everyone thinks I'm on drugs. And other times I just can't go to the dinner because I know I won't be functional the next morning when I like to write. But sometimes I go just because my wife Claudia gets sick of having me around all the time and pushes me out the door. So please keep inviting me.

4. FOLLOW UP: This is the hardest part for me. I have a list five years old of people who introduced me to people I actually wanted to be introduced to and then I never followed up. For instance, a few months ago I wrote a post "Burton Silverman, are you dead yet??"[1] Burton Silverman is one of my favorite artists. I wanted to know if he was dead to see if the value of one of his paintings had gone up. Guess what? He wrote me to tell me he wasn't dead yet. And as I type this, his studio is only a few blocks away. I could visit him right now if I want.

   Except... for some reason I never returned his email. He's on my list. But followup is my hardest part. Then I put it off until I start to feel guilty about not following up. So then I push back the follow-up even more. At my first company I hired someone to follow up for me. Claudia tells me she will follow up for me on emails. But I have a hard time letting other people do things for me that I should really be doing for myself.

   But needless to say, if you make a connection, it's so easy to *keep* it by just saying, *"hey, it was great meeting you. Lets do that again in a month or so."* Why the hell can't I ever do easy things? Instead of writing this post I could simply write an email to 400 people on my list, including Silverman. Something is mentally wrong with me.

---

1 http://www.jamesaltucher.com/2011/06/burton-silverman-are-you-dead-yet/

5. RE-ESTABLISH CONTACT: The other day I was following my own advice. I'm on the 21 Day Gratitude Diet I discuss in the post "How Being Grateful Can Make You Rich."[1] I wrote an email to an ex-investor of mine from 2004 saying sincerely how grateful I was he invested with me and I always enjoyed his advice and friendship. He immediately wrote back (because, unlike me, he's a good connector and businessman) and said, *"what are you up to? Here's what I'm doing. Maybe we can work together again."* This is 6 years after I last spoke to him. Guess what. He's now on the list I mentioned in #4 above. He's #401 on the list. But I'll get back to him. Maybe later today.After I get my driver's license. Because I promised Claudia 3 months ago that I would get it "today" although "today" means that day three months ago.

6. SHOW UP. I don't know which "rule" on this list is the most valuable. But if a good connector invites you to a dinner or a meeting, then the best thing you can do is show up. I was invited to a party of 40 bloggers the other night. The guy doing the inviting was Michael Ellsberg who recently wrote the bestseller, "The Education of Millionaires." More on him in a second. I probably should've gone. But 9 p.m.! That's like 8 hours past my bedtime. Still, I should've gone. Next time!

7. INTERVIEW PEOPLE. Back to Michael Ellsberg. This was genius. He figured he wanted to meet a lot of successful people (sort of like how Napoleon Hill did this when he wrote the bestseller "Think and Grow Rich"). So he got himself a book deal about how millionaires are educated and then, book deal in hand, he interviewed as many *billionaires* as he could find. The guy is now a MEGA-Connector. When I met him a few weeks ago he had non-stop ideas about how one goes about meeting people. He should give conferences or do coaching on this one aspect alone. Meanwhile, there's me – I blew off his party last night and didn't respond to his last email. He's on my list of emails to return.

1 http://www.jamesaltucher.com/2011/10/how-to-use-gratitude-to-get-rich/

I've done this technique to some extent. Writing for the Wall St Journal or Financial Times it was always fairly easy to get people on the phone or meet them at a breakfast. But I had a hard time following up. Anthony Scaramucci, for instance, is a well-known finance guy – running one of the biggest funds of funds and also running the annual SALT conference where guys like Bill Clinton and Vladmir Putin will speak on the same stage (Mike Tyson had to break up the fist fight). I met Scaramucci through my writing (he has also written a book) and we had breakfast together and he asked me to run a panel at his SALT conference. Guess what? I didn't follow up. I didn't even return the calls of people on his staff. Bad James!

When I was at HBO, I interviewed people for a living. The only problem is they were mostly transvestite prostitutes. But, I did get to meet the producers and creators of one of my favorite shows, "Taxicab Confessions." This was back in 1996. One of them called me recently and wanted to get together. And guess what?

8. PRODUCE SOMETHING OF VALUE: In order to connect two people, you must have people to connect. You have to meet them in the first place. The best way to do that is to produce something of value. In this post I described about how when I was broke and about to go homeless I tried a technique of just reaching out to people. I would write letters like, *"Hey, would love to meet."* That *never* worked. People are busy. Nobody wanted to meet some random guy like me. So instead I tried a new technique. For each person I wanted to meet I would spend time researching their business and come up with 10 ideas that would help them that I would just completely give for free. With one guy (Jim Cramer), I came up with ten article ideas he should write. He ultimately wrote back, *"YOU should write these"* and that started my financial writing career. It also developed a culture of exchanging ideas with thestreet that ultimately led to me selling Stockpickr.com to them. With another guy, I gave him several trading system ideas and he ultimately allocated money for me to trade. This started my hedge fund trading career.

I then write my first book about trading. Which led to Fidelity inviting me to speak at conferences, a good way to meet people. My next two talks for them are in Scottsdale, AZ and Las Vegas in the next few weeks. I've been giving talks for them since 2004. I haven't raised my prices since then because I'm always too shy to talk about money except in passive-aggressive ways.

9. TIME: I woke up for a few minutes at 3am this morning to write this list. Then I went back to sleep, figuring I'd write the post when I woke up. The last item on the list I wrote at 3am is "Time." But for the life of me I have no idea why I wrote it. If anyone can help me solve this mystery I'd be grateful.

What is the best way to get the chance to pitch your product to big corporate business? Just call up the CEO out of the blue? They don't care?
@NickHarleyNZ

The question answers itself with the healthy skepticism at the end. So I agree with what Nick is saying: you can't just call the CEO out of the blue and they do in fact care. A good recipe for failure is to have one idea that fits one business and then they will almost surely reject you, even if you get through to the CEO, which is almost impossible.

A recipe for success then is the reverse.

Have ten ideas for thirty businesses. And then move up the ladder, pitching the head of business development at each company. Or using your network to find people at the company you can pitch to.

Will all 30 respond? No! But 6 will. And 3 will want meetings. And 2 might like one of the ten ideas. And one will say yes. And that's all you need.

SUPERPOWERS

Batman or Spiderman?
@GonzaloGandia

Normally I don't like to answer personal questions (because they might not be interesting to anyone other than me) like this BUT: this is an interesting one.

Most people would say "Batman" because he built himself up without having any powers at all and became a kick-ass superhero. However, several things are very important about the batman story:

- Batman started off super-rich, which gives its own form of superpowers right from the beginning

- Batman had a track record of putting young people into tiny shorts and serious danger (the young Dick Grayson / Robin)

- Batman was so emotionally screwed up because of his parents' deaths that he was never able to have a normal relationship with a woman or any friend really. Instead, perhaps his main romance was with Catwoman, who was mostly emotionally unavailable to him and was also a criminal.

Now let's take Spiderman.

- Peter Parker was me (and perhaps you). A nerdy, shy, kid with glasses that was picked on by the cool kids, who wanted to get the girl but didn't know how.

- Peter Parker had to balance the challenges of real life (making money, having relationships, studying for school, etc) with the responsibility he chose to take on (helping people).

- Peter Parker constantly had the media against him. Bruce Wayne rarely did.

- Peter Parker got his powers from a mis-use of radioactive material. As did the Hulk, the Fantastic Four, and many other heroes created in the 60s. With the rise of the nuclear age, we must always be wary of misuse of powers we don't understand. Even with the cybernetic extensions to our personality that social media provides we must never forget that "with great power comes great responsibility" and that the challenge of remaining human in the onslaught of technology must remain utmost in our minds.

How do we gain more confidence and be sure on what we say? (In case people are trying to bring us down) @Jas_Cheng

Try as hard as you to not be around people who are trying to bring you down. Walk away. Don't engage. Don't talk to them unless needed. This part of my advice on "How to Avoid Crappy People"[1]). A few months ago I sent an email to a formerly close friend of mine saying how glad I was that he had once been in my life. He wrote back with a litany of all the reasons I was a bad person. No problem. Now if he ever tries to write me it instantly filters into the Spam box and I don't even see it. That's how you deal with crappy people (along with what I suggest in the above link)

If you have an artery that is clogged, then blood doesn't get through properly. You get heart disease and eventually have a heart attack. You might die from the heart attack.

So I'm about to explain what I really believe in philosophically. We don't have one body. We have four, and they are all mirrors of each other:

Physical, Emotional, Mental, Spiritual. And there's one "virtual blood" that flows back and forth between all of them to keep the

1 http://www.jamesaltucher.com/2011/06/how-to-deal-with-crappy-people/

whole entity (the "I") alive. If the bodies are not aligned, then the virtual blood gets clogged.

When the virtual blood gets clogged: "heart attacks" happen in one or more of the bodies. Or heart disease, or some other discomfort. This leads to self-doubt, sickness, and other bad things. When the bodies are not aligned, you can't have confidence. You can't have success. You can't get off the floor and find motivation or be creative. You can't be a beacon to others.

What power, if any do parents have to give to their children? Self-confidence?
@Pcostanzo

I wasn't a self-confident kid. I thought I was too ugly. I thought kids wouldn't like me unless I was special at something, or unless I gave them something as a gift, or unless I lied to them so I would seem more special than I am.

I have no idea what my parents did right or wrong. Certainly I know they did many things right.

But I know, for my own kids, the best way I can teach them to be self-confident is for me to be self-confident and for me to have values.

Their only comparison in life as they grow older will be their parents. If I demonstrate the right values and the right confidence then they will become the beacon to others that I hope for them.

[See also, "I want my daughters to be lesbians."[1]]

1 http://bit.ly/jdvDH2

GOVERNMENT / POLITICS

Who will you vote for President?
@TheSlycophant

I vote for "Nobody" for President. What has the President done for me lately? Any President. Name me one President that didn't increase our military presence or destroy our economy in some form or other.

Right now the US has a military presence in 130 countries and we are bombing six countries. Plus there are rumblings about war with Iran. Is this not the height of insanity? Is my way of life really being protected when we bomb and kill little babies elsewhere? And spend trillions of dollars that could have been spent to help the lives of people right here in the United States?

Here is what the President can do according to the Constitution: he can veto bills and he can sign treaties. Two things he hardly ever does. He can also MAKE SUGGESTIONS to Congress. And he can throw parties for visiting dignitaries. I think that's about it. Without looking, can you think of anything else he can do according to the constitution?

Let's not forget also: the Constitution was written before phones, before the Internet, before even the telegraph. So there was no way to get the issues out to the masses. Why not set up Internet balloting for vetoes and treaties and even all laws? People say, *"Well then 51% of the people will vote to suppress 49% of the people."* And to that I say, *"Are you crazy?"* What 51%? Instead, there will actually be discussion about the issues in a way that is not controlled by Super PACS run by Sheldon Adelson or George Soros, two people who do not have the interests of most people at heart.

My thoughts on the GOP Primary? A travesty. A circus run by the media and the Super-PACS. The final ticket will be Romney-Rubio and Obama-Clinton. And then an election will happen.

And then hopefully, no matter who the winner is, we get Google Glasses and an I-pad 8 and some more cures for cancer that hopefully the FDA, in their infinite stupidity, doesn't try to squash. Innovation will cure America. Not a President or a congressman, or higher or lower taxes. A society is made up of people. If each individual finds the strength inside themselves to take the next step, then that's the only next step for a country.

What will it take for the GOP to accept tax hike on the rich?
@ericmontas

They will never agree. Eric then asked, "That's unfortunate because how will the government raise revenues?"

My answer to that was: to raise revenues government should stop corruption, P.O.R.K. and pull back military from 120 countries. Close useless agencies (like the FDA), close various government branches (like Congress and the Presidency) and also start finding assets that they can sell and be put to better use in private industry, like national highways.

Altogether, my suggestions would save trillions of dollars. Massive demilitarization alone, which kills civilians all over the world, would save 100x more than taxing people who make over $1 million. Not that I'm excusing the bank CEOs who got away with murder in 2008 and then gave themselves bonuses but shareholders, rather than the government, need to get more active and stop that. The government has four tools to raise money: raise taxes, print money, sell assets, and spend less. I think the latter two are the best methods for the economy as a whole.

Should the government control CEO bonuses?
@StealthAviator

You mean the same US government with 9% unemployment and military actions in 120 countries and 2 major wars? The same government that can't get rid of deadlock over the debt ceilings, etc.? How many things have the government botched in the past decade? 9/11, wars in Iraq and Afghanistan with no exit strategy. Countless deadlocks, roadblocks, etc. between Congress and the President.

Why do you now want them to control salaries? How will they botch that also? Shareholders need to ultimately hold the heads of their companies responsible for misdeeds. We're going through a transforming time. Using the government will only postpone that transformation because now we'll have too many parties to blame.

I'm really disgusted with all politics and not any politician in general. This is obviously nothing new. Most people share that belief. But let's act on it. We can actually *Abolish The Presidency* and life would be a lot better.

ABOLISHING THE PRESIDENCY

Are you running for President? If so, when you are elected, would you abolish Congress and eventually the Presidency? @bgn2end

Ha, the problem with the Presidency is that at some point you have to decide that a little child is going to die at your hands (through war, military action, etc). But here's what I would do if elected and had the power to do these things

1. Abolish Congress and replace it with an Internet voting system. The only reason Congress exists is because there was no means to communicate important issues around the country when the Founding Fathers existed. [See, "July 4 is a Scam."[1]]

2. Abolish the FDA. They make lethal substances legal: most chemicals are unregulated, alcohol and nicotine are lethal,

1 http://bit.ly/kNkZ66

and they keep drugs that cure people out of the hands of old people who need that one last chance to survive. [See, "Eliminate the FDA."[1]]

3. I would abolish every cabinet position. What do we need a Department of Education for? Education in the US has only gone down since that Department was created. What do we need a Housing Department for. We had a housing crisis and nobody helped. What do we need a State Department for? Rarely or treaties negotiated and we should stop giving all of our money to foreign countries anyway. What do we need a Department of Defense for? We haven't legally declared war since 1941. If you go to Washington DC you see these long enormous buildings down every street that do nothing but bureaucracy.

4. I'd appoint myself Vice-President. Someone has to go to funerals of kings after all.

5. I'd sell off every federal asset: highways, the IRS, federal lands, trains, etc to raise money to pay down debt so that taxes can also be reduced.

6. I'd abolish the Presidency [See, "Abolish the Presidency."[2]]

A lot of people who are politically minded disagree with me on some of these things. But the reality is. If we had the bravery to do all of the above then life would be better. People still would obey Stop signs (there are local governments to handle this) and they still wouldn't kill people and "our way of life" would still be defended since our greatest offense is now global capitalism and innovation.

Who is your favorite president? @lakergodSK

There really was only one good President and the rest were failures: George Washington: He stayed above the fray of party poli-

1 http://bit.ly/q8NBdW
2 http://bit.ly/rjISwx

tics. He basically turned down a lifetime Presidency at the end of his two terms, recognizing that a country needed change and not succumbing to his own ego.

Everyone else had their shortcomings. Of course, it's easy to say that in hindsight and I'd be happy to discuss this further in the comments but who else was good? One person mentioned to me FDR but: the Depression lasted a full 7 years longer when he became President. None of his policies worked towards solving the Great Depression. None of them. He got us into WW II only after all the Jews were being demolished by Germany. He even turned away Jews who were trying to escape to America. How many Americans died once we got into WWII? He tried to flout the Constitution by stuffing the Supreme Court. He ran for 4 terms, the first since George Washington to even attempt to stay more than two.

Well, what about Lincoln? My question is: why didn't he free the slaves immediately? Isn't that what it was about? Turns out the answer is "no." He let his VP run the Union Army. And then, when the North was losing, he freed the slaves to try and get a little extra help. The Civil War was fought about the North's need to get a piece of the cotton action in the South via tariffs. Nothing else.Which is why the British (who freed their slaves in 1832) were eager to get the North out of the picture (slavery issue aside) and help the South. Money trumped the horrible sin against nature of slavery. That's Lincoln.

What is the best form of government? @MarquesDeeClairMarc

Politics is largely a scam. Here is what's important to me: I don't want people to run stop signs. Sometimes intersections are confusing. It's good when a local government figures out where those intersections are and put up stop signs. I'm not speaking metaphorically but literally. We need stop signs.

What else do we need? We don't need to go to war with anyone? I don't really think we need to give our hard-earned money to any other countries. Experiments like the Dept of Education have largely failed as have most government initiatives. What else do we need? I just don't want my kids crossing the street and then someone running them over because there were no stop signs. I'm in favor of the "Stop Sign Party."

Any political predictions for 2012? @socialhotchoco

I have no preferences one way or the other. Everyone thought Obama was going to bring peace. Instead we're bombing six countries and have military in 130 others, healthcare is more complicated than ever, taxes are killing us right in the middle of economic troubles, etc. And Bush was no better. And Clinton, Bush, Reagan, Ford, Nixon, Johnson, Eisenhower, Truman, Roosevelt, Hoover, etc. etc. was no better.

Everyone says Ron Paul has no chance even though I find him to be strikingly honest for a politician and he's winning in the polls. It reminds me of a stock I once owned. I called another hedge fund manager who had 10 million shares of it. He said, "listen, this stock is going to go from $1 to $5 and then shortsellers are going to spread nasty untre rumors about it and it will fall back into the$2s until the next move up." He was exactly right and Ron Paul reminds me of that stock right now.

I'd really like to be surprised and find a President who actually makes my life better. But I don't think it will happen, which is why I think we should abolish the presidency and take it one step further: Abolish Congress.

Then I think life will be better. But those things are not going to happen. So I never rely on politics for my happiness. Or it's outcomes.

But, like anyone, I enjoy watching the sporting event of it.

So my one prediction, whether I like this prediction or not, is:

Republicans: Romney is the Presidential candidate and Chis Christie is the VP candidate. This keeps both Wall Street and the Tea party happy and they raise a zillion dollars.

Democrats: Obama is the Presidential candidate and Hilary Clinton is the surprise VP candidate. Hilary's served her time. Biden is nobody. And Obama needs and extra oomph to overcome his poor ratings. After that, it's a close race. It's hard to unseat a sitting President.

RELIGION, MORALITY

Can you talk about morality? Is it universal or relative? @jonathankyou

Very little of morality is relative.

I did a post about a year ago that provoked some discussion on other websites. The post was "Was Buddha a Bad Father"?[1] Buddha was prince with everything: a kingdom, a beautiful wife, a newborn son.

So what did he do on the night his son was born? In the middle of the night, when everyone was asleep (so he didn't have to say goodbye) he rode off on his quest for enlightenment.

On other blogs people wrote I didn't understand the relative morality of what was happening. That fatherhood was different then. Okay, maybe. It's an interesting discussion to me.

But, more interesting to me (and something none of the other blogs commented on when trashing me on this topic) was much later when Buddha finally came to scoop up his son and teach him about life and morality.

---

1 http://bit.ly/gk1aC1

He gave perhaps his most powerful and useful sermon in all the Pali Canon (the collection of works containing Buddha's actual thoughts instead of the meassive hearsay which has gotten passed down through the ages). He basically said: *"before, during, and after a thought, action or speech, consider whether or not you are hurting someone"*

So this was a guy giving a moral rule 2,500 years ago, 12,000 miles away. This rule is still an important rule and one that many people ignore. Every day I see trolls on the Internet trying to hurt people. People in the news trying to hurt each other. Politicians and businessmen trying to backstab each other.

Nobody follows this universal rule of morality. I hope I can follow it. But it's very hard.

Notably, I believe it's the last mention of Buddha's son in Buddhist scriptures. So maybe he couldn't follow it either. I don't know.

How do you personally define morality? What is good? What is evil?
@jmorgenstern

I wrote a post about this once that nobody read. First off, I don't consider myself religious in any sense. As I write this today, it is Rosh Hashanah. I don't even know how to spell that. I'm also not a Buddhist, Hindu, whatever. But I do think it's interesting to see what texts have withstood the test of time over thousands of years.

It's the same as music. If a song withstands the test of time, compared with thousands of other songs, then you know there's something good about it. Like if a failed Britney Spears did a cover of John Lennon's song, "Imagine" then you know it would be a hit. So I am constantly reading somewhat obscure spiritual texts from a long time ago.

I wrote a post, "Was Buddha a Bad Father." The details of the post are not that important to this question but one speech that Buddha made to his son Rahula where he said, *"before, during, and after everything you do (speech, action, etc.) make you sure are not about to harm anyone, are not harming anyone, and did not harm anyone."*

In other words, he is defining Evil. Everything else is Good.

When we are good, we are on our way to Happiness. Since harming others causes undue stress. I discuss this in my latest book: "I Was Blind But Now I Can See."[1]

How do you Find Ethics Without a religion? @jonathankyou

It's an interesting question when you add the *"especially when you don't have a religion to tell you."* Ask, *"Who told Buddha?"* or *"Who told Jesus?"* or *"Who told Lao Tzu?"* I suppose you can say God did and then he asked them to transmit it to you. But I think better to find directly.

Why do people need religion? Often they get religion because they were born into it and stick to it for cultural reasons. Often people find deeper religion because they feel an emptiness or fear (of death) so they want to fill that emptiness with a path.

A path that goes from one emptiness to...another? We don't know. Better to always go from strength to strength.

So how can you fill that initial emptiness without a path? How can you make it all work out so that all paths turn around and point to you instead? I think the basic tenet that permeates most religions is DO NO HARM. It can be thought of in another way: We do three things throughout the day: we do things, we say things, we think things.

On any of these things, there's a before, during, and an after. So my one rule of ethics, regardless of religion, is: BEFORE, DURING OR AFTER, I SAY, THINK, OR ACT, I HAVE TO REALLY

1 http://amzn.to/qM8kLi

ASK: AM I HURTING SOMEONE AND, IF NOT, AM I LYING TO SOMEONE?

If your answer at any point during that above question is "yes", then stop. That's ethics without a religion.

Will you find heaven then? Will your find the end path of your religion? Who knows? But you will be happier and so will the people around you (since they won't be hurt by your words, actions, or thoughts). And when the people around you are happier, the people around them will be happier. And that's how a happy society can start. Unfortunately, most people, with religion or not, don't do this.

What are your thoughts (if any) of the expanding Atheist movement i.e.: Sam Harris, Richard Dawkins, etc.? @mczirjack

Atheism is almost a one-word oxymoron. It's an organized religion against organized religions. But they still try to keep all of the trappings of an organized religion: every "professional atheist" tries to lay out an ethical system.

I could think of myself as an atheist also – I don't believe in a man with a beard who magically created the Universe. Then I can lay out an existential system of ethics and ways for men to deal with each other without the words "under God" hanging over them.

Most people forget that Buddha was an atheist. And that even in orthodox Judaism there is no real word for God.

I prefer, for myself, to develop a system of happiness, to eliminate the constant brainwashing that occurs around me, and to try to enjoy life today.

In terms of the question: *"Do I believe in a higher power?"* I would have to answer that I do believe in the concept of SURRENDER which may or may not imply a higher power (who knows?).

In other words, many situations get so difficult you want to throw up your hands and just say, *"you know what, I did all I can. I leave the rest up to you."* And who is that you? It might be a higher power. It might be a creative force inside of you that is dying for those moments to be unleashed. Or it might simply be the feeling of gratitude that is always worth cultivating to help one find more happiness in life.

CHARITY

What are your views on how much charity one should give away, both annually and life?
@MarktMovr

A charity gives money from the interest it makes on the money it has in the bank. Part of that interest goes to administrative costs and salaries. Part of it goes to actually putting the money to work for charitable good.

So if you give $100, and the charity makes 3% interest, then maybe $2 of your money will actually go towards real charity per year. Is that what you intended?

My view is: Be a superhero.

Find situations that right now, directly need your anonymous help. Then save the world. Do it for ego reasons. Do it because you want to help. Do it because lives will be saved.

Put your $100 to work , and your valuable time to work, in situations where you can actually see the lives being saved. You will help many more people that way. Do 10% of your salary that way for the rest of your life. Lives will be saved, people will be grateful, and you will be transformed from mild mannered so-and-so to Superman from a planet in a far away galaxy.

Here is my post on the topic: 10 Reasons Why I Would Never Donate to a Major Charity or… how to be a Superhero.[1]

What do you think is the best way to "give back" to society as an individual?
@alyosha19

Everything comes from you. If you work at a charity but beat your kids at night then you have failed to give back to society. The best way to give back to society is to make sure you are healthy.

PHYSICALLY: you can't be sick and give back. You need to eat well, sleep well, exercise well. You can be your own superhero.

EMOTIONALLY: you can't give back if you are always arguing with wife, parents, etc. You need to eliminate the people from your life who bring you down and surround yourself with uplifting people who inspire you

MENTALLY: your idea muscle needs to be in superhuman shape if you want to give back to society. This means coming up with creative ideas every single day, good or bad.

SPIRITUALLY: this doesn't mean praying to an old man with a beard but it does mean having a sense of surrender and gratitude. These are two different things. Surrender is when you say, *"That's it, I've done all I can. I need help now."* Where does the help come from? Is there a god? Who knows. Maybe it just comes from a creative force locked inside of you that is dying to come out and take over the world if you let it. But it does come from somewhere. And gratitude: as soon as you wake up, list the 10 things you are most grateful for.

Then, being fully in shape, you are able to walk through life and be a beacon to others. People will be attracted to you and they won't know why. Opportunities will throw themselves at your feet. And, by being a force of nature unto yourself, you will give back to society without even directly knowing how you are doing it.

---

1 http://bit.ly/j8WikY

POKER

What did you learn from playing poker? *@GiraffesCanSwim*

At the time the question was asked I gave a 140 character answer. Something like, *"you learn quickly that all your friends lie to you all the time in order to steal your money."* But I've been thinking a little more about it.

First off, I spent 365 days straight playing poker in 1998-1999, including the night my first kid was born. Including my birthday and my anniversary. Including Christmas and Easter and whatever Jewish holidays occurred during this time.

I used to play at the Mayfair Club on 24th Street and the Diamond Club on 20th Street, both illegal clubs. The Mayfair would close at 4am and some stragglers would head over to the Diamond, which never seemed to close. Ultimately both were closed down permanently by Giuliani. I had a house in Atlantic City and would play there on the weekends. I'd go via helicopter Fridays at 5pm and fly back on Sunday night. Occasionally I would go to Las Vegas and play. This was pre-Internet poker, tv poker, and pre the big money that is in poker now.

The only time life had any color in it for me during this period was when I was sitting around a table, chips in front of me, cards getting dealt, and guys with nothing else in their lives making jokes back and forth while everyone tried to take everyone else's money.

A few weeks ago, Claudia and I ran into the guy who had once owned the Diamond Club. Oddly, we were at a party for the Wall Street Journal on some rooftop bar all the way west in Manhattan. The Diamond Club guy wouldn't give us a straight answer for why he was at the party. All he kept doing was talking to Claudia, pointing at me, and saying *"this guy was the lowest down cheap hustler there was. He's a born criminal. Watch out for him."*

I told her later he was kidding around. But the way he said it flattered me actually. Poker is a charismatic game. People who are larger than life play poker and make their living from playing games and hustling. That's what's attractive about it. That's part of what's attractive about being an entrepreneur, or doing anything where you eat only what you kill[1] and you survive in life only on your instincts.

I played because I was unhappy doing anything else. I played because I loved games. I played because I thought everyone at the table was smart and witty and I liked the repartee that was always darting back and forth. I wanted to be friends with these people. I had just sold my company, and I hadn't yet lost all my money so it wasn't the money that brought me to the table. It was the game. The charisma. The excitement. The way people adeptly played with the chips in front of them, or threw their cards into the pot when they were out, the language of motion, the gestures, the beautiful ballet of every movement in the game.

The only time I played after those 365 days was one time I went up to Murder Inc Records about ten years later and all the same guys were playing there as if they had never moved but the table had teleported over. Irv Gotti, therapper who owned Murder Inc, won about $2,000 off of me in a big pot and I left after that and didn't play again. I went to the game with Lenny Barshack who had just sold a poker sofware company.

On the way there Lenny told me how one month after he sold his company he had a heart attack on a ski slope and had officially died.

Running a company is like being mugged. When you are mugged you get a jolt of adrenalin that screams to your body: Fight! or Flight! But when you run a company its like you are constantly being mugged but you still stare at the computer all day. So the

1 http://bit.ly/pz3Mzz

adrenalin builds up with nowhere to go. All the adrenalin does is keep you alive because otherwise you'd probably die from being mugged so much.

Once the stress is over (in Lenny's case: when he sold his company) the adrenalin hits you full force. So Lenny had a heart attack one month after he sold his company and his heart went to zero for at least two minutes. Only a smart doctor brought him back to life and less than a month later we were heading over to Murder Inc Records so I could lose that final pot and then never play poker again. Poker sucks. Here's why:

Everyone at the table is your friend but they are all lying to you to steal your money. I wanted to be around these grubby guys more than I wanted to be around my wife and newborn. More than I wanted to be around real friends. More than I wanted to be around my work colleagues or my family. I don't know why. Something was wrong with me. All day long I read books about poker, and all night I would play.

I felt for the first time in years like I had a group of "buddies." Like I was one of the guys.

Here's the problem. We all were buddies but we spent the entire night lying and trying to take money from each other. You could think, *"oh, its just a game."* But I watched some of my friends go broke and cry and borrow and beg and steal. Nobody liked losing all of their money. I watched lawyers get disbarred trying to steal enough money to play poker. I saw guys escape to Israel to avoid extradition when they lost their IRS money to the poker table.

And nobody really cared about them. A guy would stop showing up and then he would be forgotten. Nobody really cared about me. We were friends. Until we weren't. And that was that.

If you find yourself playing a game all day, even Angry Birds, or Poker, or Chess, ask yourself: what might be wrong in my life? I was happy I had sold my business, but maybe I wasn't happy working for a boss now. Or maybe I wasn't happy in marriage. Or maybe I wasn't happy that all of my friends were work-related and I had lost every other friend. An addiction is a symptom. Find the real genetic roots of what is going on.

By the way, not every game player is an addict. Some people make a good living at these games. You have to judge for yourself whether you are a professional or an addict. The professionals win money from the addicts who win money from the amateurs.

As for poker itself, and this goes for all sorts of ways to making money: you want to sit immediately to the left of the dumbest, richest person at the table. He bets, then you raise – no matter what is in your hand. Then everyone else is out and it's just you and him. In the long run you get all his money. This applies to every business endeavor.

Poker is a skill game pretending to be a chance game. Many things in life are like that: sales, negotiating,[1] entrepreneurship, etc. All of these things have the element of chance in them but the ones who are skillful will take all the money from the ones who aren't. The problem is: most people think they are good because it's hard to rank yourself and many people go into denial when they lose money. They tell people, *"oh, I broke even"* when they lost money most of the night. How do you get better at any skill game:

- Read as many books as you can written by players better than you
- Study hands and the analysis of those hands
- Study and think about your mistakes. Don't regret your mistakes. You'll always make mistakes. The better you are, the less mistakes you make. The only way to get better is to thoroughly analyze your mistakes. So the more mistakes you have, the more opportunities you have to get better. Of course, this applies to everything you do in life.

1 http://bit.ly/sndKHq

- Talk to people smarter than you. Try to learn from them anything you can.

- Conspiracy theory. If you have a bad hand and someone raises you and someone then raises him, you're going to most likely need luck to win. Back out and try again later. There's a theory in programming chess computers that applies to other areas of life, including this one. It's called "conspiracy theory." If too many things have to happen in order to bring about the situation you want, then back out of it and try again later.

  For instance, if you are in love with a girl but she has three kids, is unhappily married, and lives 5000 miles away, then at least three things have to conspire simultaneously for you to ever end up with that girl. In poker, if you are facing two potential hands that are better than yours, plus you have to wait for two more rounds of betting to occur (where you can lose more money), and you are waiting for very specific cards that are unlikely to arrive, then too many things have to conspire to make the hand work. For every situation you want, determine your "conspiracy number" where you back down if that number of items has to conspire together. A conspiracy number of "three" in most things is enough for me to back down.

- Be the Bank. I was once in Atlantic City and I was playing at a table with one of the best players I knew, Joe. Another guy at the table needed chips and Joe said, *"I'll sell you some of my chips."* So the guy handed over money and Joe sold him some of his chips (an activity that is illegal in Atlantic City but it was 4 in the morning and nobody cared.) I asked Joe later why he did that. Joe said, *"Always be the bank. If you're the source of everything at the table then it makes it harder for them to bet against you."* This is a weird version of *"Give and You Shall Receive"* but it works.

In September, 1999, one year to the day after I started playing every day, I stopped. I started another company instead and lost millions at it. Perhaps then I realized that all of life is a game of high stakes poker. And on every hand you risk losing everything you've ever worked hard for. Or maybe the final thing I learned is that it's all just a game. And eventually you can just stop playing. A first kiss is better than winning any hand.

CHESS

Who was better, Fischer or Kasparov?
@StockSage1

At his peak, Fischer was better relative to his competitors than Kasparov ever was. However, if you paired them at their respective peaks (using a time machine: then Kasparov was better). Why?

- Training techniques improved.
- Computers enabled Kasparov to do quicker and more extensive research on any position.
- Kasparov was never mentally ill so he was able to pursue studies and play in tournaments for 25 straight years. Fischer maybe had 10 years of study.
- Kasparov was already recognized as a young talent at the age of 9. Fischer had to work harder to get his talent out. Kasparov also had better trainers at a young age. Fischer had none.

DRUGS

Mood-altering drugs (a la depression meds, etc.) – yay or nay? If nay then what?
@cseidholz

Clinical depression is a real physical disease and does require drugs. However, there is a severe problem.

"Depression" is a very loose, umbrella term. Does it mean "anxiety"? Or "eating disorder"? Or "post-traumatic stress syndrome?" Or ADD, ADHD, traditional clinical depression, etc.

And for each one of these things (and a dozen more) a different drug works and the rest of the drugs don't work and can, in fact, make you worse. For instance, some anti-depressants can make you feel suicidal if you are not technically depressed.

On average it takes eight years for a depressed patient to discover which drug works for them. There have been various tests that have shown this.

I'm biased on this topic because I'm invested in a company that solves this problem (so have learned a lot of the problems in the industry), CNS Response. They have 10,000 EEGs in a database. Each of the 10,000 is of a patient who was successfully diagnosed and treated.

Then, with a new patient, they match the new patient's EEG with the database to determine the right treatment. It's remarkably effective according to statistical tests done.

THE SELF HELP INDUSTRY

What is the most comical about the self-help industry? @steveroh

I think of the self-help industry much how I think of the media industry. Mildly informative if you can pluck out the gems, but mostly dangerous. Many of these so-called gurus need to make a living and so they pluck away at the fear and greed strings on the emotional guitars of their willing adherents.

Many of these people have never lost a home, lost a business, lost a wife, lost a family, and suffered real hardship but then claim the label of "coach" or "guru" and have at it. Then ten years later we hear about the sex scandals, the financial scandals, the cover-ups, the killings, the real "secrets" in The Secret.

I wish people would be honest. Instead of saying *"this is how to be perfect"* I wish these people would start from the premise, *"hey, I'm striving also. I'm trying to figure it out. Here's what's worked for me. Here's what hasn't worked for me. And, by the way, here's the screwed up crap I'm dealing with today. I hope I survive also."*

Just be honest. Is it really that hard in every industry to be honest? Particularly an industry that, first and foremost, about honesty? (Just like the finance industry should be but isn't).

Any thoughts on Eckhart Tolle? @EricRomer

Eckhart Tolle wrote the best seller "The Power of Now" and was fortunate to spend some couch time with Oprah Winfrey to really propel his message to the masses. When he first wrote the book, he printed up 3000 copies and basically went door to door at all the bookstores and handed them out. It took him years to find success, which I truly appreciate. I also think much of the advice in "The Power of Now" is interesting to read. It's a watered down version (he does not admit this) of the Hindu philosophy AdvaitaVenta (best exemplified by a teacher from 100 years ago, RamanaMaharshi) but Tolle does a good job translating that into everyday language and I agree with his approach of not mentioning the roots of his philosophy.

The one thing I think limits Tolle is that he hasn't raised a family, or failed at a business or a career, or has shared his own stories of sadness, depression, and pain. I think that ultimately limits his message. Many of have real careers that we are stressed about, family that drives us crazy, businesses that we fail at.

Many of us need to get off the floor after those failures and know that the hand that's reaching out to us comes from someone who has been there before.

WRITING

How to get over Writers Block? *@markmccarthyUK*

COFFEE. I'm just being honest. Who knows if coffee is good or bad for you. But I start writing on my third cup of coffee for the day. Since it's an addiction, at some point I will need four, or maybe five, cups to get me started. Somehow coffee gets my brain over-stimulated and ideas start to happen and then I write them down.

READING. I always read before I write. This morning, for instance, I read some William Vollmann (an essay he wrote about writing), some Bukowski, some Miranda July (she has the breathless "love me" way about her), Michael Hemmingson (who was writing about William Vollmann), and a little of my all-time favorite author – me. When I'm reading I often get ideas about what to write. No idea is totally new. So if a writer experienced something I've experienced or makes me think of something I've experienced, I can repackage it and spread the love in my own, hopefully unique, way.

As an example, the other day I was reading Tim O'Brien's short story, "What We Carried" about the physical items he and his fellow soldiers carried into the jungles of Vietnam and how they also carried emotional and mental baggage.

Well, for me, going into NYC, working to support my family, trying to struggle against the competitive fire of everyone else trying to take money with their grubby fat hands during the course of my day, reminds me of that. So I wrote about what I carry during my day. Did I copy him? Of course, but it's also my truth and not his.

SAME TIME EVERY DAY. If I wake up at 4:30, and done with my reading and coffee by 6, I'm sitting in front of the computer trying to write. Your brain is your slave, not your master. So if I tell the brain every day that at six AM he has to jump through hoops and ride an elephant than he better do so. (Or maybe he is a "she." Can a man have a female brain? Sometimes I think I do.)

START IN THE MIDDLE. This is the best technique on the list and will always work If you have a topic already. The other day I was writing one of those *"7 Things I Learned from X"* sorts of posts. I was staring at a blank screen. I couldn't figure out the intro. So I said to myself, *"how about I just start with the list?"* I then wrote: *"1) Honesty"* and then I couldn't think of what to say underneath honesty so I went to #2, then #3, etc. Now I had a list of seven things but no descriptions/reasons for each item and NO intro and NO conclusion. But I also had NO PROBLEM because the content was done. So I just filled in the blanks like a game of Mad Libs.

START WITH THE BLOOD. This only applies if you have a topic. I wrote a few months ago "5 things I learned from Isaac Asimov." Or maybe "10 things." I forget. But when I think about Asimov and me the first line that stands out is, "The first time the police were ever called to get me was when I was 15." From there I have a story and will lead into the 5 things, particularly when I follow "D" above.

DON'T EVER TALK ABOUT WHAT YOU'RE GOING TO WRITE. When a piece of writing is inside of you it's like a baby that's growing. The baby is feeding off of your vitality, your brain, your emotional strength, and over time it grows. If you talk about it, then you've given birth. I've given birth to more dead babies than I can count. Give birth on the written page first. Then you can talk about her as she matures.

INSPIRATION. Sometimes I get hard-core writer's block. I did my reading, my coffee, my analysis of my big past failures, etc. and I can't figure out something to write. I do several things then to look for inspiration:

I look around my room: This inspired "The Tooth," and also "The Ugliest Painting in the World," and also "Is Burton Silverman Dead Yet."

I go to some websites that always have intriguing photos that might inspire me: Boingboing.net, Brainpickings.org., thebrowser.com, extragoodshit.phlat.net (warning: explicit), etc. For instance, "7 Things I Learned from Louis Armstrong"[1] came from the first item on the list above.

My own material. I look back to stories I've written and see if there's a way I can slice it up further. For instance, I've written about starting a company in the 90s called *Reset*. But I never wrote about selling it so here I wrote about that.

The most embarrassing things. I had hard-core writer's block one weekend. So I picked the most embarrassing stuff you can possibly write about and just spewed it out in a post called, appropriately, "Writer's Block."

---

1 http://www.jamesaltucher.com/2011/07/7-unusual-things-i-learned-from-louis-armstrong/

MAKE YOURSELF THE BAD GUY. If I'm writing about the love of my life I can write *"I broke up with her with a text message to her phone."* Or you are writing about how to make money you can start with, *"The worst thing I ever did was steal money from my parents."* Then that leads to: why you stole, how much you stole, what you did with the money, how you found a more honest way to make money, and what those 7 ways of making money are. Voilà! A post!

HONESTY CHECK. Make sure you're not trying to protect yourself. Protecting others is important. Do No Harm. But if you're going to tell a story, it doesn't have to make you the hero. For instance one of my more popular posts was "How I Screwed Yasser Arafat Out of $2 million." Right off I said I needed $100 million. Nobody needs $100 million.

Then I described what I would do with $100 million, everything I did to try and get that hundred million, and ultimately what Yasser Arafat had to do with it. The story told itself. But I was arrogant, foolish, a bad guy, and at least at that time, had no idea what I was doing. If I tried to protect myself in the writing then there would've been no story. So always do an honesty check. Are you saying something because it's true or because you are trying to protect yourself?

SOLVE A PROBLEM. If I have a problem like, "I'm angry" then I have at least two delicious courses that will make a full meal. 1) What am I angry about? 2) How I deal with the anger. This not only solves my problem but I think gives the world a little advice on how to deal with anger. So how do you do this? Look inside your stomach. What's making you feel a little sick or inspired today? Your job? The prospect of being an entrepreneur? Jealousy of Larry Page? It can be good or bad. But it has to be inside of you so you can get it out, analyze it, kill it, destroy the beast, and solve the problem.

The above ten techniques have basically produced every piece of writing I've done this year plus five books. Now my only problem is I promised Claudia I would cook fried chicken for lunch and I have no idea what to do. I might fake it by going to a restaurant while she is napping and getting fried chicken from them and pretending afterwards that I cleaned the whole kitchen. Sometimes I get away with that.

Where do you see yourself in 5 years? @ClarkCovington

I honestly don't know. I need help figuring that out. I write every day and post on my blog about 3-4 times a week. I enjoy it. I'm also in a bunch of investments, private and public.

I'd like to figure out the next steps with the blog, if there is one. I've rejected all advertising. I don't know what to do. But if anyone has ideas what else I should be doing I'd be happy to hear them.

How do you find the time to write and exercise? @GlobalMacroZen

The only answer is *"wake up earlier."* We waste so much time during the day. For instance, checking email is a 2-3 minute adventure. Many people check email on their phones or computers at least once an hour. That's 32 minutes a day. About 10,000 minutes a year. Over a 40 year period that's 400,000 minutes or 277 days checking emails.

Other time wasters that can store up minutes in your day: watching dumb primetime TV. Going out drinking with friends (have coffee with your friends mid-day). And there are a million other time wasters that can be read about in any number of productivity books. What do you do with all this extra time? Easy. Go to sleep an hour earlier. Wake up an hour earlier, refreshed (no prime time junk in your brain).

This seems like not a big issue in your 20s and 30s. But when you get older you realize that a minute of anger, a minute of stress, a minute of junk is 60 seconds that you could've been happy.

If you don't exercise, if you don't get the creative muscles going and stay healthy, then when you are older all of that junk adds up: you'll be less happy, less healthy, quality of life will be down.

@GlobalMacroZen then said:
"my schedule won't allow that."

Is that what you are going to say on your deathbed?

Is it possible that a small improvement can be too small? No. Improvements compound exponentially and add up to great success over time.

Someone just wrote me, for instance, and said they want to write a novel (they have the idea) but don't know how.

The answer is really simple: first practice staring at a blank screen for 20 minutes a day. Then start writing 500 words a day. A novel is 60,000 words.

500 words a day is 180,000 words in one year (and that assumes breaks for 5 holidays). 500 words is only 2-3 paragraphs. So you can write 3 novels in one year. Or one good, highly edited novel. And that's if you limit yourself to 500 words.

With practice you'll go up to 1,000 words, 2,000 words, etc. Any small improvement (staring at a blank screen to get used to the idea of writing) will add up to success beyond belief (who would think you can do 3 novels in a year so easily?)

What are the most important factors in succeeding in financial journalism?
@dyer440

I can write a book on this one topic. So here's my top 8 points on succeeding financial journalism:

SCOOPS ARE NO LONGER IMPORTANT. It used to be if you had a scoop you had at least a 24 hour lead on all the other news sources so scoops actually meant your circulation went up and business improved. Now, because of the Internet, any scoop has a 1 second lead at most on its competitors. So chasing scoops is a waste of time.

HELP PEOPLE UNDERSTAND COMPLEX ISSUES. Break it down in easy to understand language. Why did Italy cause such a panic three days ago and then manage to borrow $150 billion no problem the next day. It's because the headlines are just trying to scare people. Fear has replaced scoops to drive circulation. Then it becomes a race to the bottom, who can scare people the most.

MY PERSONAL RULES in 9 years of writing for financial sites (and creating a site with millions of users, Stockpickr.com, which sold to thestreet.com in 2007):

- Always create value. Can people use your article to have a better understanding of the markets

- Provide analysis and proof. Don't just give a random rant. Give real numbers to back things up.

- Be honest. If you're wrong, you're wrong. But don't just cave in to whatever the current panic trends are.

BUILD YOUR NETWORK. Everyone's got a story. As your network of contacts grow, the value of it grows exponentially. The network will be your source of interesting stories.

POSITIVE AND OPTIMISTIC, because in the long run (like for the past 200 years) you will be right.

TELL A STORY. Don't just give numbers. Tell a story of where the world will be five years from now and how we will get there, starting with the events happening today. As the story develops into the real world, you will have the fuel for more and more stories/articles.

BE A LITTLE VOYEURISTIC. Everyone wants to know about their heroes. Who are your heroes? Why are they your heroes? What are their "secret origins"? Write about them and follow their stories. Many journalists have made a living off of just Warren Buffett.

DON'T TRASH ANYONE. A lot of well-known writers disagree with this. They lose in the long run. And the long run is all I try to care about.

Note: I stole #1 from a discussion with Kevin Ryan, who is one of the founders of Doubleclick, Gilt, and financial media site, Businessinsider.com.

How can a humor writer bleed? *@idiotlaureate*

The only thing humor writers do as bleed. Bleeding is about sharing a situation that we can all relate to: usually disgusting, embarrassing, and humiliating, and finding the truth in it. Some examples from some of the funniest people around:

Sarah Silverman's book: "The Bedwetter: Stories of Courage, Redemption, and Pee" (right in the title).

Paul Feig's book: "Superstud: Or how I Became a 24 Year Old Virgin" (Feig is director and writer of the show "Freaks and Geeks" and has directed many funny movies)

Comedian Mike Birbiglia's book: "Sleepwalk With Me: And Other Painfully True Stories"

David Cross ("Arrested Development", "Mr. Show")'s book: "I Drink for a Reason"

Jim Norton (super comedian): "Happy Endings: Tales of a Meaty-Breasted Zilc"

Artie Lange: "Too Fat to Fish"

And so on (I also recommend Ellen Degeneres's three books and Judd Apatow's collection of stories he found funny).

Starting out as a writer, how much time should I budget daily to reasonably get going?
@Bmp135

The most important thing is consistency. Every day. Seven days a week. Writing is like a muscle. You start to get writer's block more frequently when the muscle atrophies. I've been writing consistently since 2002. Before that I wrote consistently from 1991-1995.

Nothing good, mind you. Just writing. But, I've also read a lot of books on writing by well-known and successful writers. Here's the general consensus that I've experienced myself and all the writers I have read seemed to have lived by:

Three to five hours a day, every day.

Walter Mosely (one of my favorite mystery writers) has written that if you just write 500 words a day (three paragraphs) then in 100 days you have 50,000 words. Which is roughly the length of a small but publishable novel. So you can write 3.5 novels a year. Or write one really good one that you've rewritten quite a bit. Try it.

One of my new year's resolutions is to try it.

What is your writing schedule?

I try to do this every day: Wake up at 4:30am. Coffee. 2 hours of reading. What do I read? I try to read strong autobiographical fiction.

That sort of sounds like an oxymoron: "autobiographical fiction." But authors like Bukowski, Raymond Carver, William Vollmann, Miranda July, Mary Gaitskill, have strong literary voices precisely because they write about what they know best: themselves. They dive deep and even if they tweak their own biographies enough to produce fiction, it's often the fiction that is heavily based on truth and their own lives that comes out the best. Jonathan Ames, Michael Hemmingson, Donald Ray Pollock, Don Carpenter, John Fante, Celine, are also in this category. I like to get my mind buzzing with their voices to get inspiration.

Then I write for 2-4 hours, then rewrite.

When I'm writing, I have to search the feelings in my body to see what 's bothering me. If something pops up, I immediately start writing what's bothering me so much that my body hurts to think about it. Then I keep going and see where it takes me. [See: "33 Unusual Ways to Become a Better Writer"[1]]

I also find that if I don't stick to this routine then I usually can't write for the day. It's the same time every day. And if I miss a day, it probably takes me two days to get back into the routine. I was busy this week in a lot of early meetings. It totally threw me off. Now I'm back!

Is the hardest part of writing a novel getting started? @MichaelComeau

I like Walter Mosley's recent book on "How to Write a Novel." It's a short book because his main advice can be summarized in one line: Write 500 words a day. A novel is about 60,000 words. So in 120 days (4 months) you have your first draft write. 500 words is only about three or four paragraphs.

Something else I read on a blog: a woman who writes (and publishes) many novels (she writes serials about, I think, vampires) explains how she writes 15,000 (!!) words a day. She outlines heavily beforehand. And then she just goes for it. She says she went from 1000 words a day to 15,000 words a day using this technique.

Then, both writers say this is only for first draft. And then you have to rewrite. But whatever, the first draft seems hardest to me.

1 http://bit.ly/gDzHGb

BLOGGING

Am I crazy to give away free plumbing advice on my blog? Will that sink my company?
@OconomowocPlumb

It will make your company a huge success.

I've made a good amount of money on five different occasions. (I've also lost a good amount of money on at least 15). But the one thing in common on all five occasions is that I gave away free advice.

In my first company I sold, Reset, Inc. our job was to make websites for companies. The way I landed almost every customer was by spending time with them and giving them complete free advice about how they could improve their website. On some occasions I even recommended competitors. On other occasions I never got the client. They took my advice and did it themselves. Heck, we lost our biggest client that way at one point (until they had to come back for more "free" advice).

Let's not forget: the only thing Google ever does is give out free advice. You can say to Google, *"I have Hepatitis"* and Google will say, *"I can't help you but here are ten of my competitors (other websites) who can help you."*

Then when you have another problem who do you go back to? The source of the fount of free advice: Google.

The Bible says, *"Ask and You Shall Receive."* There are two parties there: the person asking, and the person being asked (who then does the giving). The person being asked (in the Bible) is God. I'd rather be in the position of the person being asked then the person asking.

When you emulate the properties of the person/God being asked then your business will grow faster than you can even handle it (as happened with Google when their free advice became the best on the planet).

So *Give and you Receive*[1] should be the rule to live by. In fact, it's the title of one of my favorite posts I've written.

How can I get people to my blog? @Rita_Colbert

I would suggest:

- Keep reading quality writing so you can improve the quality in your blogs.

- Tell more honest stories in your blog. Bleed so we can see what you are really made of. Don't just say "10 tips to success." Share an intimacy so we can be intimate.

- Guest post on other blogs and link back to your blog.

Storytelling has worked for 5000 years. It's not going to stop now just because we have blogs and tweets. Rita is definitely doing some good storytelling.

How do I pick a blog name? @rbinmn

Use your own name. It's the best way to spread the word about what you are, who you are about, and what you stand for. Look at Huffington Post. The most successful blog ever (whether one likes it or not – it started as a blog) was built on the back of one person's name. Someone should make a libertarian version of the Huffington Post although lewrockwell.com is doing a good job.

1 http://bit.ly/fi1mHC

Is there one simple, common feature, one element you aim to achieve in every blog post?
@rajlikes

In every post, try to do these three things:

1. Bleed. Sharing intimacy is a way to connect with people. Share an intimacy you are scared to share. That is bleeding.

2. Tell a story. If your post is just "top 10 ways to be a weight-lifter" then nobody cares. You have to tell your personal story of how you went from a 98 lb weakling to a Charles Atlas weightlifter. Remember those ads in the back of comic books? In just a panel or two you go the story. The 98 lb weakling was at the beach with his girl. He got sand kicked in his face. He got angry, he did the Charles Atlas method, and now he's ripped and shredded like Mr. Universe.

3. Deliver value. Since I started writing I make sure I deliver value in each post. Has to be value you can't find anywhere else. There's seven billion blogs and articles posted every day. How does your feeble words stand out amongst all that. You have to deliver huge value. See, "33 Unusual Ways to Be a Better Writer."

Thoughts on the anti-blog movement of authors using email services like MailChimp? Direct to the inbox as they like to say
@Unpacktherat

TV didn't replace movies. Movies didn't replace radio. Radio didn't replace reading. Photography didn't replace painting.

People chose the medium they want to create in. The key is to have something to say. Then figure out the medium you want to use to say it. I like blogging because, for me, it seems like hard work to build out an email list when I don't feel I need to. Anyone can just come to my blog and read what I have to say plus I can have other links on there to other posts that I think are relevant. I like my posts to be "3 dimensional" and link all around.

But some people like email lists. It's more direct. I would say the style is a bit different. So it just depends what medium you want to be a creator in, an artist in.

The key, again, is to have something to say. Then create.

What should I blog about? I change my interests every day. @tfrojd

Don't give yourself anymore excuses to not just sit down and create! Creation takes practice and time. So start now whether you have consistent ideas or not.

Set up a blog: "My New Interest"

Every day or week post on it. Completely tell me about your new interest:

- Why are you interested in this new thing?
- Why did you lose interest in the old thing?
- What connections are there between the new and the old (or older?)
- And tell me at least one new thing about your new interest that I could not have read anywhere else.

Eventually you'll start to see themes arise across your interests. Those themes will intermingle. Something cohesive will come out. For a brief time, you'll be a blogger, then an artist. Then you will create something new out of the intermingling and mating of all of these interests.

SELF-PUBLISHING

Do authors need to know about marketing? @ReadHeavily

A friend of mine was visiting a publisher who had published a book of mine. Now they wanted to publish my friend's book. She asked them specifically: "What marketing did you do for James Altucher's book?"

They answered, in all sincerity: we got him a review in the Financial Times, a segment on CNBC, and an excerpt in thestreet.com.

Here are the facts:

- I had a column in the Financial Times! I wrote my own review as a joke.
- I had a regular weekly segment on CNBC. I used one of those segments to promote my own book.
- I wrote 3 columns a day at the time for thestreet.com. I used one of those columns to do an excerpt and nobody complained.

So that's the "marketing" that publisher did for me.

Here's the truth about book publishing now: there are only two characters in this grand production: the writer and the readers. Everyone else in the middle: booksellers, agents, editors, packagers, distributors, marketers, etc is in massive upheaval and transition and they are seldom willing to admit it. Book publishers don't provide anything.

Here is my "Why and How I Self-Publish."[1]

---

1 http://bit.ly/kKRy6d

If I were a book publisher I would transform myself instantly in the following ways:

- Reduce the lag time from book acceptance to publication from one year to one month. There's no such thing as a "catalog" now. Just get the book on Amazon and bn.com and if the book does well the small bookstores will start calling.

- Become digital marketing agencies. Learn how to use social media to really start the discussion on books. Zero book publishers have done this correctly although they think they have with outdated email lists that generate zero sales.

And as an author, the main thing I can suggest is: read my link above about self-publishing but also take control of your own marketing:

- Book public speaking engagements where you give your book away for free.

- Syndicate blog columns related to your book content on popular sites related to your content

- Engage with twitter, facebook, google+ to have an active discussion (throughout your life) about how your book's content is important to you. If you believe in what you are saying this is not "marketing" but "honesty and sincerity."

The sincere voices will always rise to the top. Oh, and also Snooki will rise to the top.

Where will e-books be 5 years from now? @eradke

I was at a dinner sitting next to "Binky" Urban (the most successful literary agent in history) and Tina Brown, publisher of Newsweek and The Daily Beast, among other things. I asked them both about the future of publishing.

Self-publishing

Urban said, *"Publishing is doing better than ever. I've seen more 7 digit advances for first time novelists than ever before in the past six months."*

Tina Brown said, *"Book publishing is dead. Its all e-books."*

I think they are both right.

But I know my own behavior:

Behavior #1: I go to a bookstore, pick out all the books that look interesting to me, and then sit down on a chair right there in the book store and buy them on my kindle app on my i-pad. Amazon benefits and not the bookstore. Maybe this is not fair but this is how I do it.

Behavior #2: I no longer publish with traditional publishers. I self-publish in both kindle and e-book. And most of the sales (I can see all the numbers) come from the cheaper kindle version.

This is related to another question asked me but I'm self-publishing another book within the next four weeks: "I Was Blind but Now I See" about how to break down the myths that we are bombarded with every day so that we can find success and happiness. I'm going to use the same technique to self-publish and probably launch the book by giving it out for *That's* my behavior. But before long everyone will be free at Barry Ritholz's Big Picture conference where I am speaking.

Here's the key:

- Write 500 words a day on the topic you are most passionate about, on your business, on whatever you want.

- Within 100 days you'll be ready to self-publish

- Self-publish

- Now your book is your business cards. When everyone else is handing out flimsy little cards with email addresses you'll be handing out a book. For better or worse, you'll stand out. And that's what you want.

What would you do if you meet Stephen Covey down a dark alley? @IndustryKeyword

Ha-ha! I assume this was asked because for the past three weeks Covey's book, "The Seven Habits of Effective People" and my book "I Was Blind But Now I See"[1] have #1 and #2 in Amazon's Kindle store for motivation.

The only big difference is: his book was published 20 years ago and he's still #1. Stephen, won't you let anyone else have a chance? To be fair, I was #1 for one whole day before he recaptured the throne.

And so my answer is I would congratulate him. He clearly had a message that resonates with time. I can only hope to be eventually so lucky as to help as many people as he has helped.

I did write a post about his #1 habit and my experience with it. I view all the rest of the habits he has as corollaries of the first one.

Also, my book isn't so much about "effectiveness" but "happiness" – how you can tear away the shades that keep the room dark, so the light can flow in.

Do you ever struggle to simplify and structure complex ideas when writing books? What steps do you go thru? @iAspin

Yes, every single thing I write. In my last book, most of my ideas in the second half come from texts I've read that were written over 2000 years ago. I totally plagiarize them. But they are texts that have withstood the test of time and I know, when written with

1 http://amzn.to/rbiL9r

modern examples and modern language, that they will still resonate and people will still find Truth in how they can apply these principles in their own lives.

But if I were to just cut and paste them, they wouldn't be useful at all. So I run them through the filter of what's happened to me in my own life and how I've used these principles and it becomes much more accessible.

How do you make money selling an eBook while giving it away at the same time for free with a special offer? @CLAcevedo222

You can't make money selling books. Well, some can. JK Rowling can. The Freakonomics guys can.

But that's one in a million. Literally those are the statistics. So here's why you write books (if money is your motive):

- Everyone acknowledges that a book requires expertise and hard work. That expertise can win customers.
- Consulting engagements
- Speaking engagements
- More people see your name which can lead to more networking. Networking can bring you down a maze of opportunities totally different from where you started but much more lucrative. Tim Ferriss, the author of the "4 Hour Body" has Twitter shares, for instance. How did that happen? Because he knew how to make money off of his books!
- Or, if you are prolific, you can write ten books. You can write 100 books. You can write 467 books! See, "5 things I learned from Isaac Asimov."[1]

---

1 http://bit.ly/tyiEXj

So, go write a book! [See also, "Why and How to Self-Publish a Book"[1]]

Do 1 star reviews on Amazon affect your writing? And would you rather get a 1 star review or a 3 star review? @BenNesvig

Ben has just self-published an excellent book. It's really funny.

The only problem is: he only has five star reviews. What's so bad about that? I, for instance, hate when I have a one star review. It kills me. It makes me question my entire existence. Someone actually read my book and thought so poorly of it they took the time and effort to log onto Amazon and spend a precious few minutes trashing my whole life in view of anyone. But that's what sells books. When people are arguing, that's controversy. Controversy sells. The #1 book on the Kindle has 81 1 star reviews (and 3000 5 star reviews). But the top-rated Kindle book, with 697 five star reviews and zero reviews of any other sort, is ranked down at #10,000 in the kindle store. So thank your one star-reviewers. They will drive more sales than your five star reviewers.

A few months ago I read the excellent short story colletion "Knockemstiff" by Donald Ray Pollock. Afterwards, I read the reviews. Some were one star reviews and when I read why it showed they had totally missed the point of the book. But I wrote Pollock to cheer him up and told him the one star reviews were almost better advertisements than the five star reviews. All the people offended by the "sex and violence." Hell! I'm a buyer when I see that.

Is it possible for you to make a living from your self-published books? @ailon

Yes and no. There are all these literary-fab stories of some 17 year old writing zombie novellas making $1 million a year. That's great if you can do it. It requires persistent writing, blogging, reaching

1 http://bit.ly/kKRy6d

out to audience, being in a hot area at the right time, etc. But, most areas are not like that. Most people are not like that.

The way to make "make a living" money from self-published books is to treat the book like an enhanced business card. You write it, you parlay it into expertise validation, which gets you consulting and speaking gigs.

And you can write more books. You get to pick yourself instead of having some random publisher pick you, edit you, and delay your book coming out for a year where you end up making the same amount of money anyway. I did four books last year. My self-published books made me more money.

IS IT TOO LATE?

Is it too late to start all over at 47 and still make it big? @tombakalis

The answer is, *"of course not."* There are so many examples.

I can start off with this one I wrote about. He started his career in his mid 40s and became a billionaire.

But there are many other examples:

- Laura Ingalls Wilder (author of "Little Women") published her first novel at age 65.
- Colonel Sanders (who was only an honorary colonel) started his first KFC at age 65. Sold it in 1964 for $2 million when there were 900 of them.
- Tim Zagat started Zagat's at the age of 51.

- Raymond Chandler's first novel came out at 51.
- Rodney Dangerfield was a used-car salesman well into his 40s before switching to comedy.
- Gandhi's political career started at age 61.
- Frank Mccort wrote his first novel in his 60s.

And so on.

Focus on having high quality of life into old age. You have to plant those seeds now. Then today's 50 is yesterday's 25.

Take for example this article I wrote the other day about a guy who started his career over at the age of 48 and went on to become an international success:

I asked Rodney Dangerfield what was the craziest thing he ever saw at three in the morning. Without skipping a beat he said, *"Her husband came home!"*

We talked some more. He was more somber than I thought he would be. He told me how he was an aluminum siding salesman and then when he was in his mid 40s he got sick of it and he was depressed. He had a mid-life crisis. He decided to get back into comedy (he had utterly failed at it in his 20s). When he was 48 he started the comedy club "Dangerfields" which became the biggest comedy club in NYC for some time. From aluminum siding salesman to comedy impresario at the age of 48. He had all the best comedians perform there. *"I'm the one who first had Jim Carrey perform!"* he told me

We talked some more but I forget the conversation. I remember being obsessed with one thing, telling him how inspirational it was that he made a change so late in life (I was 28 at the time and even then wondering how it can be possible to switch careers) and totally changed the direction of his life, career, everything. He seemed proud of this and would tell more stories of the change.

Afterwards, I was standing on the sidewalk watching him walk to his car. George Carlin, who I had to interview next, leaned over, pointed at Dangerfield, and said, *"that guy is totally high right now."* Of course I'm name dropping. I'll tell you one more thing about George Carlin. One time I went to see him perform at Radio City Music Hall for an HBO special. I took a date. She casually mentioned some guy she was friends with.

Being hopelessly insecure, I asked her if she "liked him." She got a disgusted look on her face and said, *"how can you even ask me that?"* The lights went down then, the show was starting. And then for the rest of the show I didn't pay any attention and I was upset that I had blown it with her. I don't think I laughed once at anything George Carlin was saying.

Then later, people who watched it on TV kept saying they saw me in the audience. Apparently a friend of mine was doing all the camera work and he told me, as a joke to me, he kept going right in close on my face for audience reactions. And since I was upset the entire time the reactions were not good.

Oh, one more thing. My friend doing the camera work once told me, *"I have a pickup line that always works but you can never tell anyone."*

I said, *"ok, no problem. I promise I will never use it or mention it to anyone."*

We were in his office. He had hours and hours of videotape of Ultimate Fighting Championships so that was on in the background. Ultimate Fighting usually involved one guy pinning another guy down very quickly so you couldn't see what was happening as the guy on top broke one finger at a time of the guy on the bottom even after the guy had already pounded the floor, signaling "stop."

I have another story where I had breakfast with the guy who ran the Ultimate Fighting Championships (the girl who I went to the George Carlin event with introduced us) but that's for another time.

"So tell me the pickup line," I said.

It only works on girls from Canada, he said. But if a girl says *"I'm from Canada,"* you ask, *"Really? What street?"*

At a talk I gave in Canada once I used that line and they all sort of groaned. Don't use that if you are actually IN Canada.

Back to Rodney Dangerfield. I can't think of a single movie or appearance of his I didn't like. *Caddyshack*, when it came out with Dangerfield, Chevy Chase, and Bill Murray, was the funniest move I had ever seen at the time. *"Back to School"* was hilarious. And so on.

I liked how his humor was so instant and spontaneous. How he could immediately look and act completely crazy. His humor was not only physical but he had a catch phrase that seemed particular to him while he said it but was something we all instantly relate to, *"I get no respect."* This ultimate self-deprecation catapulted his career for decades.

But he was also an inspiration. That you can go from being an aluminum siding salesman in your 40s and you can be, frankly, hideously ugly and look like nothing is going your way ("I get no respect" comes from experience) and then starting from scratch become one of the biggest comedians and box office stars ever is inspiring to me.

There's lots of things that I wanted to do in my twenties that I never succeeded in. Writing a novel, for instance. I wrote four or five (depending on how you define "novel") and sent them around to dozens of agents and publishers and got rejected everywhere. I wrote a comic book script for the DC character "Delirium" and never got a response. I was inspired by all of Alan Moore's and Neil Gaiman's comic books and read every comic I could but it wasn't enough. I wanted to be a PhD in Computer Science but was thrown out. I wrote a spec script for "The Larry Sanders Show." But nothing. I tried shooting two documentaries. I even had as a New Years resolution last year to try standup comedy but it's hard when you go to sleep by 8pm every night.

But anything can change at any time. A few years ago I was having coffee with a friend of mine whose book was being published the very next day. He was depressed. *"Sales are going to suck,"* he said. *"This is it for me."* It was his third or fourth book and the last one had not sold well.

No way, I said, this will be a bestseller.

But I was just being encouraging. His life changed overnight (the book was Freakonomics) and his career is still catapulting upwards in ways that I'm sure are still surprising to him when he wakes up in the morning.

Every day we wake up a new person. We can forget that and too easily reattach to our past: *"I'm too old. I'm too ugly. I didn't get the right education. I don't live in the right city. I don't have the right contacts. I don't have any skills. I don't know how to even get started."* And so on. We give ourselves excuses so we can continue our life of depressive misery.

Rodney Dangerfield was clinically depressed all his life. He took medication (often self-medicated) for depression every day for the last 60 years of his life. He had every excuse to never make any changes, including the all-encompassing one, *"I get no respect."*

Today I'm going to download Caddyshack, his first big hit. He was not supposed to be such a major character in it. But he steals every scene. I haven't watched the movie in maybe 20 years. But it made me laugh. Every day I want to leave my life open for changes. I want to stay one step ahead of the excuses that try to drag me back down into hell. But today I want to laugh.

RETIREMENT

How should one choose when to retire and where to live? @Elyiggy

The simple answer is: never retire. People die within two years of retiring on average. So unless you want to die, why retire.

But transformation is another story. After spending 45 years as a janitor at the pencil factory it might be time to try something new. Presumably the entire world is open to you. Your kids are grown up. You might have some savings, etc.

The key is personal freedom. Being able to do what you want, when you want to. Assuming your health needs don't require you to be in one specific place, pick a location where cost of living is incredibly low and live out your life doing your fantasy work. What's your fantasy work? For me it might be scripting comic books. It might be doing these Twitter Q&As. I can do these from anywhere.

Maybe when I retire I'll move to India where I can live for about $500 a month at most.

Or a friend of mine just told me about rental prices in Savannah, Georgia, which he said, "is the most beautiful place in the country." And rents and cost of living sound about half of that in the New York City area.

Here's the three step retirement method:

1. Transformation. Sharpen the idea muscle and start brainstorming what else you can do. Play in a jazz band? Open a café? Open a used bookstore? Start a website? Write a novel? What the hell do you really want to do? The world is open to you.

2. The world is open to you, part II. With your current savings plus what you can make in your transformed job (and assume three years of living before you make a single dime at your transformed job), where's the cheapest place you can go that still fits your minimum needs of comfort and beauty. Explore the world a little. It's your oyster. You can live anywhere.

3. Do it.

CHARLIE SHEEN

What are your thoughts about the scene from Wall Street when Charlie Sheen sits in his apartment with beautiful girl and says life is great?
@Julian_Lenz

A lot of times we strive for things that we think will increase our happiness: sex with the beautiful person at the gym. More money. A lot more money. A house. A nice big house. A nice car. Winning that last hand of poker, etc.

But think about all these things: you have sex with the beautiful woman one day (happiness!) and the next day you're wondering where she is when she doesn't return your calls (unhappiness!). You make a lot of money on a deal (happiness) and then you lose it on the next (misery!).

This is not real happiness. It's a mountain: the entire time you are walking up you are sweating and in pain. Then you get to the peak and you look around and you're happy. And then you go down the mountain you no longer have that same happiness.

This "peak happiness" is not real happiness. It's a fake happiness. It's a dopamine addiction created happiness.

OCCUPY WALL STREET

What is your stance on Occupy Wall Street? @KarimGuessous

I think a lot of people, including myself, have been badly hurt by the financial crisis that occurred in 2007-9 but really began in 2000-2002 and can be argued, began much earlier.

The problem is this: I used to live right on Wall Street. So I know the people who actually work there. Many of those people lost their jobs, their pensions, their homes, their savings, their 401ks, etc.

I hate to think now that along with all that they already lost they have to deal with thousands of people shouting at them and shoving signs in their faces as they try to get to work. A shit job they have to go to feed their families.

I understand "Wall Street" is symbolic but the reality is that "Wall Street" moved to Park Avenue between 45th and 57th Street many years ago. I used to live in the same building where JP Morgan worked (it got converted to rentals). Now Jami Dimon, the CEO of JP Morgan works on 45th Street near Park Avenue. And the hedge funds are all in Greenwich, Connecticut. And the SEC and the Federal Reserve are in Washington DC. Why protest in the face of hard working Americans when the real culprits who should be put on trial live and work elsewhere.

Here is the thing. OW!

That's what the Occupy Wall Street people are feeling. They are in pain:

- They lost their jobs

- They lost money while rich people got bonuses

Occupy Wall Street

- They lost their homes
- Maybe they lost their families

All of the above happened to me. Specifically in 2008. I could easily be down there protesting for the same reasons.

But, I actually lived there for several years. On Wall Street. My roof overlooked the New York Stock Exchange.

You never saw a sorrier, sadder group of people going to work every day than on Wall Street in March, 2009. The actual people who work on Wall Street are low-level people who are slaves of the banks. These people lost everything. Now, to top off their depression, the protestors are waving signs in their faces as if the Wall Streeters are the guilty ones.

Let me tell you something: the guilty parties live in Greenwich, CT. Work on Park Avenue and Washington, DC, and they are more than happy to see Occupy Wall Street all the way downtown on Wall Street.

Because of the lack of organization, the Occupy Wall Streeters think they are protesting something symbolic: the greed of Wall Street. The rich bankers are 5 miles north laughing their way to the bank.

Let's get the banks to start lending again. Let's let the stock market go up instead of protesting it. When there is more money in the system, more people will get hired, more people will find opportunities, more businesses will get funded. Being angry at the people who lost the most won't help anyone.

99% OF THE COUNTRY DOESN'T CARE ABOUT OCCUPY WALL STREET.

Clearly people are angry. 9/11. The dot-com bust. The housing bubble (which provided for housing for many people who could not otherwise afford it) followed by the bust (all of those people then lost their houses), the Lehman crisis, the financial and unemployment crisis, the government bailouts that didn't seem to have any check at all on CEO compensation. Heck, I'm angry. And filled with regrets over this past decade and what I could have done differently to avoided some of the pain that spread throughout the country and world.

But, let's keep the pain in check. It's time now for people to clean their own house before barging in and cleaning everyone else's house.

Furthermore. Every decade our quality of life gets better. The bottom 99%, the top 1%. All 100% gets better. Literacy goes up, lifespans go up, violence goes down, the number of families with two cars goes up (and the number of car deaths go down), etc.

Someone once told me, *"Don't look at what's in my wallet and I won't look at what's in yours."* The same thing here. Okay, CEOs took too much money. That sucks. Bush and Obama gave them that money. It was horrible.

But now is the time for recovery. Get healthy first. That's your choice about whether or not you can get healthy: physically, emotionally, mentally, spiritually. Build your health. Be a beacon to those around you so they can be a beacon to those around them.

There's been horrible violence in these Occupy movements and there's been no real demands. If you want to do some good in the world, get healthy, start a business (or manage one) and make your business do the right things instead of the horrible things that have happened this past decade. Become a leader, not a protestor, an innovator, and not someone peeing in Zucotti Park (a park where many people I know (chess players, food vendors) have had their lives disrupted negatively by these protestors of graduate students.) Now is the time to move on and be successful and show the CEOs of last decade how it's done. Don't blame them or the government on your own failures. Now is the time to succeed.

What's up with the Wall St. protestors and now that it's gone global? What is their objective? @StealthAviator

The Wall Street protestors are angry. They are so angry it hurts. Let me tell you an example. A good friend of mine has a credit score of 817. Which means he's not only returned every penny he ever owed he probably gave the lenders even more money and said, *"hey, go have a big party or something. I'm paying for it."* I've never even met someone with that credit score. To be honest, before I spoke to him (yesterday) I thought the top score was 800. But he says he has 817 so I believe him. He also made 300k last year. He wants to buy a house for 500k and put 30 or 40% down.

Guess what? The banks won't lend to him. The banks have $1.6 trillion in cash. The banks CEOs took home about a trillion in bonuses since the bailout. And yet they won't give my hardworking friend a loan so he can live in a house with his wife and three kids.

And that's the cream of the crop. There are a thousand stories of foreclosures, layoffs, etc that are much worse. So people are angry. I get it.

But nothing the protestors do are going to change the banks. It's like all the people who protested the Vietnam War at the Democratic Convention in 1968. Guess what! You won. Nixon got elected. You were protesting the wrong thing at the wrong place and towards the wrong people to get what you wanted accomplished.

The banks want to make money. They want to lend to people.

I can go two ways from here: personal or public.

I'll do public first:

- The Fed needs to stop paying the banks to hold onto money. The Fed was so paranoid that the banks were going to lose all of their money that they started paying the banks 0.25% to hold onto their reserves. Why would the banks lend that out?

The Fed should just get out of the way. By the way, the Fed is located in Washington DC.

- Why did we give any bailouts without some restrictions on executive compensation? By the way, Congress and the President are in Washington DC.

- There are 6mm private small businesses in the US. Instead of randomly printing money and giving it to the defense industry ($3 trillion already spent in Iraq and Afghanistan – two countries I still can't find on a map if you had a gun to my head) why not do one single little stimulus that incentivizes each of these 6mm small businesses to hire one more person? Bam! Unemployment solved.

And now, more importantly, the personal:

- Why are you so angry? Corporate America has always sucked. Think how much better it is now than a century or so ago before child labor laws. Women garmentos would go on fire and the bosses would keep them locked in until everyone died. Children would work 80 hours a week for pennies. Heck, we had slaves.

- If you want to walk comfortably, you can't cover the entire world with leather. You put on sneakers.

- Get my post out: The Nine Ways to Succeed (which really should be called "The Nine Obstacles to Success"[1]) and start following them. Start being grateful for what you have. Start being the smartest person in the room.

- Plug all your leaks. Anger, even if justified, is a leak. I get scared also. I'm scared every day. I don't want the world to end. I want to have opportunity for myself also, and my daughters, and their daughters. But that means I have to work at it. The banks will never give it to me. Eventually a boom will come again, like it always does, and the banks will throw money at

1 http://bit.ly/jxz9pM

> all of us. But first, let's get ready to take it and this time, let's not lose it.

So what about those big CEOs who took the bailout money? Should they be put in jail? Who knows. Why did Washington DC give them that money? I don't know anything. I'm only worried about what's in my pocket right now. I don't care about Obama (other than that I think we should Abolish the Presidency) and I don't care about Lloyd Blankfein (other than that he didn't return my email several years ago but that's another story). I worry about what's in my pocket, not yours and I trust will consistently do the wrong thing, like they always have.

THE DAILY PRACTICE

Which of your daily practices is most important to your creativity?
@JulioD

I threw up all over the floor and my two year old said, *"throw up."* I had just had a steak dinner with two investment bankers. I was trying to pretend I wasn't quickly going poor. But I was sick. I was sick in body, mind, soul, and even then my marriage was probably falling apart and I was losing my house. My two year old was probably scared seeing me on the floor with puke everywhere.

How do you get off the floor? How do you keep the universe excited and surprised by your mere existence? Every time I would do so I would end up back on this floor. I hope now I've learned my lesson. I pray I learned it.

But everytime I've been on the floor I've applied the principles that I describe in this post.[1] In order to be creative you have to be healthy physically, emotionally, mentally, and spiritually.

1 http://bit.ly/fuiRS9

All of them are equally important. For instance, how you can be creative if you are so sick you are throwing up? Or if you are constantly arguing with wife or friends or colleagues (the emotional side) or you are mentally sluggish or if you are spiritually unable to surrender to the creative force inside of you.

Sometimes things are so bad for me I have to give up, I have to surrender. I have to say, *"what the hell, I've done everything I can, now I need some help."* Who are you surrendering to? It might very well be that creative force inside of you that's saying, *"please let me out so I can run rampant throughout the universe."* It doesn't have to be god you surrender to but everything inside of you (your creativity) that you never knew existed.

So everything is equally important. If one leg is missing then the chair will tip over and fall down.

How many minutes each day do you meditate? @TodayTrader

The word "meditation" is almost a bad word. Americans don't like to sit around and do nothing. They also, as a group, don't like new agey-stuff, or Eastern philosophy or anything that puts a hold on the religious freedom which allows them to work hard, make money, and enjoy the fruits of their success.

But the brain whirs around all day long. It can't stop: why did she says this? Why did he do that? How much money do I have left? Where can I get a new job? And on and on. What a drag that we are stuck in this constant stream of thoughts, unable to sit by the shore and just watch them go by.

Meditation implies a few moments a day where you can sit on that shore and watch the thoughts. But rather than limit it to a few minutes, how about a way to meditate all day.

In "The Power of Negative Thinking" I describe a meditation technique that I use to try and meditate every second of the day. I think it's hard for most people to sit for 20 minutes a day and try to shut everything down. Better to train yourself every day to be mindful of what you are thinking and drain yourself like a wet dirty sponge of all the negative thoughts that plague us without stop.

How does one become a faster decision maker while still maintaining the quality of your decision?

In one of my posts someone said, *"you're always pushing 'The Daily Practice,'"* but the fact is, when I was down on the floor, going broke, losing my home, losing family, losing friends, losing businesses, any number of times over the past 25 years, the only things that's lifted me up is simultaneously getting physically, emotionally, mentally, and spiritually healthy.

Imagine that you have four bodies and not just one. And there's an invisible blood that flows back and forth through each body, the way blood flows through your physical body. If any of the bodies or out of balance, then this invisible blood will not flow. And you will start to feel it. You'll get less healthy, your relationships will sour, your ability to have ideas and execute on them will turn to crap, your ability to surrender and find balance in your life will falter.

But when everything is in balance and the invisible blood is flowing, when the heart of your being is pumping without any impediments, then you will make decisions faster, better, smarter.

What is the single most important thing to do today, right now, to move towards a better world? @ReadHeavily

I wrote about this in my post "How to Change the World" and one of the commenters said it best. *"Mother Theresa said if everyone swept in front of their house then the end result would be a clean world."*

The thing you can do today to make the world better is to make yourself better. By the end of the day can you look back and check these boxes:

Physically I took care of myself (I exercised, ate well, didn't drink, slept well, went to the bathroom, breathed in fresh air, etc)

Emotionally (I didn't dance the dance with anyone who wanted to engage me in a negative way. I expressed gratitude and love to the people who loved me).

Mentally (I used my brain to come up with ideas, to make people laugh, to stretch myself outside of my comfort zone in some way).

Spiritually (I was grateful to be alive. I am humbled to be alive. The pain I sometimes feel is not the same as the "real me" but something that gloms onto me unsuccessfully).

If you can do that then the result will be:

You will be better. So one person out of 7 billion is definitely better. That's the first step on changing the world.

The people immediately around you will be better. They will be inspired by your presence. They will want to act with integrity and awareness around you.

Then the people around them will want to be better. And so on.

So you improving yourself ends up having an exponential network effect on the world around you. There's no better way to change the world for the better.

If you are angry at something (bank CEOs, Bush, Obama, etcetc) then the only thing that gets spread is anger. I've never seen that in thehistory of the world change anything for the better.

Anger creates Hitlers.

Is there such a thing as righteous anger? (Example, being outraged at Joe Paterno)
@Theopaulson

Anger and fear are twins out of the same evil womb. "Righteous" anger only dresses it up in pretty clothes.

Example, a lot of the Occupy X crowd (both the protesters and the police) are being fueled by anger. There is over 1,000 documented cases of violence, antisemitism, anger on both sides. Both sides feel righteous.

The USA felt righteous when it invaded Afghanistan. Thousands of civilian (and 18 year old military people) deaths later and ten years later we're still there. Did our righteous convictions win? Do we feel better now? Is the world safer? Less corrupt?

I can't thing of any case where anger is righteous or justified. Let's say your boss yells at you, for instance? Should you get angry back? That's probably the easiest strategy if you want to get fired. But you're never going to win an argument against someone who is angry.

Best thing is to walk away and then come back and talk when he is more rational, or quit if he is permanently irrational, or just do the best job you can with a horrible boss.

Let's say your spouse cheats on you. Will your anger be justified? It wont' change the past. You should then figure out what the best thing to do is? Move out? Divorce? Address the issues that caused the betrayal (it always takes two to tango so no reason to get angry when you also are at fault).

Fear, jealousy, anger, envy are all mirrors of each other. Better to calm those tendencies, to be aware of them (being aware of anger is the easiest way to change it from a flame to a simmer).

I know from my own experience: anger has led to me getting fired, having bad ideas, not completing things, not sleeping, wasting moments when I could've been happy, building bad businesses, and on and on. Better to avoid, no matter how "righteous."

JAMES' FAVORITE THINGS

What TV shows are you watching these days? @perfectweapon

Louie, Rome, It's Always Sunny in Philadelphia, Mad Men, Shameless, Arrested Development (on iTunes), In Treatment, Entourage. Any others that are out right now I should be watching? Do tell me.

I read non-fiction voraciously but want to read some more fiction. What novels could you recommend most highly? @importgenius

I used to be like that. But then I realized that most non-fiction writers have zero writing skills so it's hard to actually get through one of their books. I really like fiction writers that have strong autobiographical voices so I can learn from not only their stories but also the strength and quality of their literary voices. Here are a few that I re-visit often:

- "Ham on Rye" by Charles Bukowski is the novel of the 20th Century in my opinion. See: "6 Things I Learned from Charles Bukowski"

- "Jesus' Son" by Denis Johnson is the best collection of short stories.

- "No One Belongs Here More Than You" by Miranda July.

- "Anything" by Raymond Carver.

James' Favorite Things

- "Whores for Gloria" by Willliam Vollmann (or Rainbow Stories by him).
- "I Never Liked You Anyway" a graphic novel by Chester Brown.

Start with those and you've started with the best fiction on the planet in history (in my opinion)

What are your top 3 favorite movies? @authenticvoytek

I have more than 3 favorites. BUT:

- Lawrence of Arabia
- Gandhi
- Schindler's List

Why those three? Because they are all epic, they are all terrifying. They are all roughly true stories (the Truth is often a 1000x more interesting than fiction).

And they all deal with people who have a certain degree of craziness. People who through their personal nobility, their hardships, their inner demons and angels, rose up and created an entirely new world from that nobility and craziness. Whenever I see one of those movies, I want to be like the main character, someone with the inner strength to change the world, to change everything around me with the force of my will. That's what those movies are about.

Plus, in those three movies, the cinematography is without compare. Even Lawrence of Arabia which is so much older than any modern special effects movie today. The desert landscapes are beautiful, and the pace of the movie, the music, the language, the acting, all fit the pace of being in a desert – slow, thirsty for more, beautiful. And Lawrence is so insane, so crazy, and yet so determined to be a leader among men. To shine where he was not allowed to shine in the strict confines of the class system of England. Ditto for the other two.

BUT: I have to add now:

"The Conversation", "After Hours", and my all-time favorite comedy: "Superbad" as runners-up.

What are your favorite self-help books? @YoavEzer

"Self-help" is a weird phrase. I don't like most of the self-help industry and here's why: it's 1000s of books written by people who have experienced mild failure and little success but they want to make million crowding that section of the bookstore. So who are they helping? Also, when you look at recent self-help books (a lot of the authors mentioned in "The Secret") they seem to be doused in scandal. Who needs it?

Also, what are they helping you do? Many self-help books are about making money. I'm convinced before you can truly make money (and keep it, and be happy with it) you have to first make sure all the energy is properly flowing inside of yourself.

So instead of recommending anything that is on the bookshelf I'm going to recommend a few public domain titles:

1. "The yoga sutras of Patanjali" are not just for people interested in yoga. The text is from 300 BC and contains 195 lines. I think what was happening is that Buddhism was stealing so many adherents of Hinduism that it provoked in a very marketing-like fashion, a response. So this guy, Patanjali, basically repeated what Buddha said but added a few more things ("sitting straight", which led to yoga) and more on breathing (which led to the study of pranayama).

   My post, "How to Deal with Crappy People" was based on Chapter 1, line 33 of the Yoga Sutras.

2. I recommend the Lojong Slogans written in the 12th Century AD. It was a set of 59 lines used to transmit Indian Buddhism to Tibet. And basically discussed how to work through the things that plague your soul (similar to many self-help books today). Pema Chodron (a popular self-help writer today from the Buddhist tradition) bases much of her work on these slogans.

3. More contemporary. Wallace Wattles book, The Science of Getting Rich (written in 1900 so is public domain) is the basis for most self-help books afterwards (even Napoleon Hill's "Think and Grow Rich" from 1937 is based on Wattles' earlier works and "The Secret" is almost 100% based on it). Wattles approach is very serious: money is good, never think about poverty, and only think about getting rich. Never worry about your past, never talk about it, never associate with anyone who can bring you down. Only think about being rich and how good that will make the world.

   - If I had to recommend one contemporary guy I'd pick Eckhart Tolle's "The Power of Now" or "A New Earth." While he mentions Jesus frequently in his book his work is very much based on a sect of Hinduism called Advaita Vedanta and mostly based on the work of a guy named RamanaMaharshi.

OTHER FAVORITES:

Several people asked me my favorites on a variety of topics so I supply them here:

FAVORITE VONNEGUT BOOK: "Slaughterhouse Five." The most autobiographical – it details Vonnegut's experiences in Dresden during and after the fire-bombing that destroyed the entire city. It shakes up Vonnegut's spirit to the point where the main character can't even stay fixed in time. The book is surreal and I think represents Vonnegut's purest voice and philosophy.

FAVORITE FREAKS N GEEKS EPISODE: The 14th episode. "Dead Dogs and Gym Teachers." Specifically the scene at the end when

Bill is crying because he can't handle the fact that his mom is going out with the coach of the school. Bill is the ultimate geek and he scorned the coach and everything he stood for. I related to Bill and felt like crying when he was crying. Also, the first scene where food is falling out of his mouth while he is laughing at Garry Shandling (one of my favorite comedians) is classic.

FAVORITE BOOK ABOUT SOFTWARE: You don't have to be a programmer to appreciate "Joel on Software" by Joel Spolsky or "Hackers & Painters" by Paul Graham. Both guys are (or started as) programmers, built up successful business and learned how to apply their programming skills to deeper issues in both business and life. I recommend both.

FAVORITE BUSINESS BOOK: "The Rational Optimist" by Matt Ridley is the perfect book for business. It shows with science and sound reasoning why the doom-and-gloomers will always be wrong. Economic development has saved country after country from the disasters of infant mortality, illiteracy, war, terrorism, and so on. I also like "The Science of Getting Rich" written in 1900 by Wallace Wattles.

FAVORITE BEATLES SONG: "While My Guitar Gently Weeps" – by George Harrison, the most underrated Beatle and perhaps songwriter among the four. Even the title is like an entire poem by itself.

FAVORITE SUPERHERO: Dr. Strange, of course. Not only is he the Sorcerer Supreme but he cleans up on women. I mean, look at Clea. And he has magical powers that can basically do anything: teleport, create exotic food fishes, heal people. He can also astral project, something I've wanted to do since I was 12. And he's got a guy named Wong who is a master or martial arts who is his assistant.

What is your favorite chapter in your last book? @ClaudiaYoga

Ok, she's being sneaky. She's my wife. Bad Claudia! Now you force me to self-promote. And I even heard your giggling while you were typing that tweet so you aren't fooling anyone.

But it's a good question. She knows people will think my book might be just a collection of blog posts and she wants me to always describe how it's different.

I constantly recommend "The Daily Practice" to pick yourself up when you find yourself on the floor and are having trouble getting up and started again. In this book, in the chapter, "What is True Happiness and Success" I provide a lot of modifications to that practice that's not anywhere on the blog.

Also, in the introduction I provide an overriding arc which suggests that the first step in success is acknowledging how much we've been brainwashed, who has brainwashed us, how do we get over the brainwashing, and then from there what are the steps needed to be truly happy with our lives. I think these are useful chapters. At least, they have been for me. As I say in the conclusion, *"Don't believe me. Try these things for yourself."* And then see what happens.

OTHER BOOKS BY JAMES ALTUCHER

- How to Be The Luckiest Person Alive My first self-published book.
- The Altucher Confidential – (The first blog to be turned into a comic book).

FAQ ME

- I Was Blind But Now I See

I WAS BLIND BUT NOW I SEE

Here is the first chapter of "*I Was Blind But Now I See*":

When I was six years old about half my first grade class was Jewish and about half were Christian. I was born and raised Jewish. As part of that, we always learned (through friends, school, family, etc.) jokes about Jesus. Similarly, the Christians had jokes about the Jews. We would whisper these jokes amongst ourselves but occasionally some would get out. I remember one time at lunch we had all just about had it.

It was time to fight. Jews versus Christians.

At lunchtime we were all running around, pushing each other down to the ground, throwing dirt on each other and shoving each other. Nobody got really hurt.

Finally one kid yelled, *"Wait!" And we all sort of stopped and looked at him. "Wasn't Jesus Jewish?"*

Someone else said, *"Yeah!"*

The first kid said, *"How about we compromise for the Jews to just agree that Jesus was a great teacher and then we don't have to fight."*

And then after that we didn't fight.

But why would six-year-olds care enough about something 2000 years old to fight about it? It's because from an early age on, we're brainwashed about almost every single belief we hold dear.

I Was Blind But Now I See

I've believed in so much that it has ruined me. For example: I believed that marriage would lead to a happy life. That $100 million in the bank would make me happy. That going to a great college and graduate school would make me happy. That having a TV show would make me happy. The becoming a chess master would make me happy. That having a lot of sex would make me happy.

The list goes on and on of the things I thought that would make me happy. Each of the above, and 100 things more, made me so desperately unhappy at different points and yet I still fought for them, fought to control what I couldn't have in a world where I became desperately needy for everything I couldn't have.

Happiness starts when we have the freedom to pursue what's inside ourselves instead of the myriad joys and pursuit's and successes that are outside ourselves.

How do we find out what happiness means so we can start to really pursue it? I describe "The Daily Practice" in my last book and also in this book. In this book I provide much more material on it. I provide modifications and more descriptions to make it flow more smoothly depending on how much time one has to commit to it and also to explain it even more deeply than I have done before.

This practice and the techniques used in this book have worked for me. I have been able to come back from the dead. To live with my fears, to conquer my anxieties (most of the time – every day is a process), and to continue striving for success and happiness. Note I didn't say I "found" success and happiness. It's a process that continues every day. And tomorrow when I wake up again I have to apply these principles again. But every day I move closer... to what? That's it. Just closer.

Why have I been writing the blog at jamesaltucher.com?

I want to show what a fool I've been: in business, in dating, in sex, in marriage, in fatherhood, in friendship. And not just once. Many times I've ended up broke and lonely and lost. So lost I've had to simply give up all hope of finding my way back or I would've gone completely insane.

I've also been writing this blog with a tiny bit of sleight of hand. Often when I write about the *Nine Obstacles of Success* (as an example) I'm not necessarily equating Success with money.

Money is an important step towards happiness because it buys our freedom. But when I write about creativity or how to eat what you kill, it's not only because I want you and I to have a lot of money (and we will as we follow those chapters) but to have freedom, to break down the brainwashing that chains us, and ultimately to find some happiness. Money doesn't bring happiness. But it allows us to spend more of our waking hours pursuing happiness once we have it. It's only a step towards happiness. I've stated before but will state again, MY ONLY GOAL is happiness

But first we have to figure out what happiness is? Because the brainwashing is so deep we're convinced that going to Harvard, getting a home, voting, getting married, is what leads to happiness. It is not.

We then think: getting more money, having more success, having fame, could lead to happiness.

It does not. We can still have all of these things. They certainly help get you the freedom to pursue happiness. But they are not the means. Just part of the process we will learn how to accomplish here.

So we have to build up our definition of "what is happiness." Then avoid the obstacles to that happiness.

And so, let's say then one achieves this elusive goal. The next step is to make sure it lasts more than a day. That it builds, that it enraptures us and helps us to enrapture and free the people around us.

BUT FIRST we have to retrain ourselves from the outside in. And then from the inside out.

What does that mean?

It means take a look at the beliefs you hold dear. For instance, a belief that is hard to analyze is that *"it's important to have a college degree."* Or it's important to "vote." Or it becomes important who we vote for. And what they stand for. Or that some wars are "justified" while others aren't. We're taught from an early age what's important and what's not. When I say "early age" it's from so far back we can't even remember. Your false training starts when you are swimming the breast stroke down the birth canal.

For example, if you are feeling a little agitated as you hear the *"importance of voting"* belief challenged in the previous paragraph, or any of the other examples, if your blood is suddenly boiling or you feel the need to tell me off, then perhaps you are observing firsthand the depth of the profound conditioning. Looking in is a hard job, not for the faint of heart but rather for the warrior at heart. It takes courage.

We're exposed to over 10,000 ad and brand impressions every day. Each one of these imprints further programs the brainwashing we've been subjected to.

BREAK IT ALL DOWN

We still have a chance to start over. To have the openness and sense of wonder and eager curiosity of a one-year-old while having a fresh mind that is not controlled by the external programming.

So our definition of happiness has to unravel like peeling away at an onion. And we're going to cry along the way. You can't help it. Getting to unveil your own beliefs is transformative. You will be different. Your parents, colleagues, friends, lovers, might not be happy about it. They may be weary of it, distrustful. You'll be the one-eyed king in the land of the blind and that will suddenly put you in an uncomfortable position with everyone who is still being brainwashed.

This is a good thing. It means more opportunities for success. For money. For better understanding of yourself and the world around you. For better opportunities for real happiness. You're breaking free. Now you have to stand alone, where previously you stood together, but this is where opportunity is created. Now you can see past the valleys, and over the horizon something beautiful and new awaits.

From then we have to rebuild the interior. The plumbing got all screwed up. We gambled our happiness that the exterior promises made by our elders, advertisers, governments, teachers, our friends, were real and fulfilling. But the tide has come in this past decade, things have changed, we are in a whole different beach and we're all standing around looking at each other naked.

So we have to think again. We have to put on new swimsuit's, and learn to swim again. We do this by building the muscles that have long atrophied. The physical muscles, the emotional muscles, the mental muscles, and the spiritual muscles. We figure out new tools to light up our creativity, to fight fear, to eat what we kill. To hustle and then exchange society smarts with street smarts."

THE 10 COMMANDMENTS OF JAMES-ISM

By the way, replace the word "James" with your own name. "Claudia-Ism" or "Phil-Ism" or "Jane-Ism," or Pierre-ism or Mario-ism, etc. You have to believe first in the many complex layers of yourself before beginning to subscribe to the beliefs of others. You need to get to the core of you and what you believe before you accept what others say or think. You have to stand on your own two feet, be your own teacher, your own light.

1. Acknowledge that every day of your life you are brainwashed. Just like when we were kids we believed in Santa Claus and how George Washington chopped down the cherry tree, now as adults we've been trained to believe in much more danger-

ous and insidious ideas. Being aware that you need to question everything is commandment number one, including, by the way, questioning what I'm saying to you right now.

And then on top of the brainwashing we suffered in schools, from our parents, from our friends, from society, there's the 10,000 ad impressions each day that hit the periphery of our eyes and further tries to tell us what little intricacies of life will deliver goodness and happiness to us. We can't even begin to be happy until we at least acknowledge that SOME brainwashing has occurred. And the more we examine this brainwashing, the more we will see how in other ways we didn't even expect, we've been programmed like little robots.

2. Who brainwashed you? Parents, friends, teachers, government, media, entertainment, advertising, the education system, the banking system, and organized religion. In that order although they are all interrelated.

   It's not their fault. And there's no reason to be angry at them. They were brainwashed also. Everyone is just trying to survive the best way they know how. And there's been generations of mental programming combined with now trillions of dollars of advertising dollars that keep everyone in line. It's a massive recruiting machine that tries to keep us from our true happiness by redefining happiness in various ways that are inaccurate and even harmful.

   From here on in, we have to realize that the plane is going down and we have to put the oxygen mask on our own face first. The mega changes that occurred in the past 10 years turned the world upside down; we are in a different planet now, one that requires adapting, new ways of thinking, and of breathing. So get on your own mask, see how it feels. Breathe again.

3. What can you do about it? Take one belief at a time, turn it upside down. Learn how to break down your beliefs. Be your own rebel. Take, for instance, the belief that *"going to college*

leads to a better life." Try to understand why you believe that. Who told you that was true? What happens if someone told you the opposite *"that NOT going to college would lead to a better life?"* Does that thought disturb you? Why does it disturb you?

Some of these beliefs are so sacred inside of us that it really feels like punishable blasphemy to believe the opposite. I know this because I've had death threats and angry emails over almost every belief I've ever challenged on my blog (examples will follow later).

The goal is not necessarily to believe the opposite of all the things we've been programmed to believe, but to separate out who we are from our beliefs, so that we can truly examine them, scrutinize their roots, and be able to look at them from all 360 degrees instead of just the acute sharp angles that have been shoved at us almost since birth.

Let's shed our labels. People want to be in the "tea party" or they want to be "environmentalists" or "democrats" or "republicans" or "a homeowner" or a "graduate." Let's shed all labels for a little bit while we inspect them. Maybe they are all good labels to have. But there's nothing wrong with re-examining them under a new lens.

It's understandable that we want to be part of the pack, the herd. The flock feels protective. But we've learned now that it is most likely a bag full of false protections.

The past decade has been such a hard decade in many ways. 9/11, the Internet bust (and tech depression), the wars, the loss of tens of millions of jobs, the housing crisis, the financial crisis. We know, for instance, that the myth of corporate safety was just that – a myth. People who worked at corporations for 40 years were fired without severance or benefit's. This happened. I don't mean to say *"the only one you can rely on is yourself"* because clearly the people who love us are valuable to us. But at the end of the day, happiness comes when we escape the robotic constructs built to house our beliefs and become real humans, and stand in the light.

I am also NOT advocating going it alone. Nobody can do everything alone. That is not only arrogant it is plain dangerous. But examining our own beliefs gives us a solid ground from where to relate to others in a more honest way, and create more effective relationships that provide better results in the new environment we find ourselves in. Honesty with yourself is the first step towards challenging the beliefs of the mega-system.

4. Happiness is the ONLY goal. We don't have to know what happiness is yet. But we know this: we don't want to be sad or fearful anymore. We don't want to be anxious. We don't want to do things that cause us to feel guilt. That's a start.

   Think about it, when you say you want to have more money, why is that? You may answer that you want it so that you would be able to travel some more, or have more time for your children. And why is that? You may say because then you would see the world and write that novel you always wanted to write, or teach your kid to throw ball. And why is that? And you may say, because then I will be happy. So why not go for "happy" in the first place? Why the long route when there is a shortcut? Certainly money buys some degree of freedom. So getting more money is a reasonable goal. And we'll get it. But let's cut out as many intermediaries to happiness as possible.

5. The obstacles of Happiness are sickness, inertia, doubts, laziness, carelessness, vacillating, lack of progress, delusions, and falling backwards. Each of those allows us to fall back into our brainwashing and stop ourselves from challenging the world around us so we can break down our thoughts and see things as they truly are.

6. The path to happiness involves being as healthy as we can: physically, emotionally, mentally, and spiritually.

7. Physically. We can exercise, we can try to eat healthy, we can sleep eight hours, we can avoid alcohol and other foods or liquids that are either hard to digest or will later inhibit the brain cells we desperately need to enjoy quality of life in our elder years. This is hard. I'm not advocating being a vegan, or a weight lifter, or a yogi. Just being aware. When I was younger I could eat five Big Macs a day. Now if I eat more than two meals a day it becomes much harder for me to digest and clean my system. I'm 43. It's important for me to make sure when I'm 83 I'm still healthy and able to explore the things that make me really happy. The root of almost all physical ailments as we age is what we put into our intestines (and lungs).

8. Emotionally. I'm a pretty angry guy. I feel a lot of people have wronged me and, it's not just a feeling – a lot of people have wronged me. I also have a lot of regrets. A lot of things have happened to me that are my fault that still make me sad. But dwelling on this does neither me nor them any good. You can't be healthy if you obsess on the crappy people or events in your life.

   Also, fear is an important topic here. We try so hard to control the world around us. Will it give us money? Will it get us the girl? Will it get us the job we want or the promotion we want or will it get us the customers and allow us to build the business we want? These are just a few of the things I often wake up first thing in the morning afraid about. Fear gets in the way of finding out what makes us happy. You can't be happy if you're stressed. Controlling the world and have it going your way will only lead to a temporary happiness. What happens the next time the world goes a different way? Then you aren't happy anymore.

9. Mentally. Your mind needs to be as sharp and creative as possible. You need this for two reasons. One is so you are creative enough to achieve the success and money that will allow you to pursue and purchase your freedom. Two so that you can train the analytical parts of your mind to break down all the

myths that we hold true every day. I have several chapters on this.

10. Spiritually. This word has a bad connotation. It sort of smells "new age-y." Or like organized religion, which many people despise and have rebelled against. But what I really mean is "Surrender." If you wanted the Earth to move out of its orbit from the Sun, you would give up. You can't do it. You would try (somehow, I don't even know how you would try) and then finally you'd say, *"I give up. I can't do it."* In general, life is like that. We have dreams, most of them don't work out, and we can either continue to force those dreams into place, or we can give up. Giving up doesn't have to be a sad thing. It's a transition. It's a little death (a term often used to describe an orgasm).

    Sometimes you're just on the floor, failure has slashed you again, and all you can do is look up at the sky and say, *"You win. I give up. Tell me what you want me to do and I'll do it."* And you hand yourself over.

    To who? Not to God. Not to an old man with a beard living up in the sky. But deep inside you there is a creative force that desperately wants you to succeed, wants you to make a lot of money, wants you to fall in love and be happy, wants you to do these things not so you can live in exotic mansions and travel the world fifty times over, but so that you are free from the constraints of a normal job and can pursue the real exploration of what and where is the happiness around you.

Follow these ten ideas with discipline (described more throughout the book) and you will make more money than you know what to do with. This world is filled with money. The global economy is over $50 trillion dollars. You only need a tiny speck of that to have the freedom to quit your nine to five job where you are totally exploited, so that you can then take a breather, live a long healthy life, and pursue the things that really make you happy.

If you are just a little more creative, emotionally healthy, and physically healthy, than your competition and you avoid the nine obstacles, then that money is eventually yours. Money is the most external manifestation of the spirituality that's the tenth commandment above. It stems from the fabric of your core beliefs. Smart and strong subtle beliefs lead to the clarity and efficiency that can make riches manifest.

Follow these ten ideas and you will start to have the relationships that bring you up instead of down. You will have the creativity to bounce from idea to idea to explore what's real in your brainwashing and what isn't. Ultimately, you'll change and you'll change from being robot to a human, from a zombie to truly alive.

You'll look around and see all of the zombies with the glazed look in their eyes, their angry anonymous thoughts flaring through their heads, their desperation and neediness for more money, more sex, more of anything that will make them forget what their real goal is

For every one of us that clicks and comes to "know thyself" a thousand others follow. The zombies can see the light once you become the beacon. Everything that was a zombie in you will shed away, like the bandages that covered the mummy, until finally a real human will stand up. Others will notice, some may hate you, some will be curious; some of us will get back to swimming happily in the new ocean.

That human will look straight at the sun for the first time with eyes uncovered by bandages. And the sun will be so happy to see you she will smile right back.

What is this book?

This book is divided into two parts. First, looking at the ways in which the mega-recruitment machines have hypnotized us into believing what they wanted us to believe: so they could take our money, fight wars, convince us that we were safe while they took advantage of our hard work in exchange for that myth of protection.

I bring these things up not to convince you that they were all WRONG. I could care less what they were.

Nothing I say in this book will change anything that happens on the outside. Wars will still be fought. The recruitment machines, funded by billions of dollars, will continue to run their assembly lines of zombie creation. You and I can't stop that. Fighting with a pig only makes you muddy and the pig happy.

But I bring them up to show how looking at the beliefs we hold dear can be examined under a microscope, and perhaps even modified inside of ourselves so they don't have as large an effect (e.g. they stop taking our money so we can use that money for other means – like buying our freedom and pursuing more individual dreams instead of the pre-boxed sets that they so beautifully wrapped up for us).

That is Part One.

Part Two is when we get into the nitty gritty of what happiness really is and how can we find it. Two sources try to tell us what happiness is:

- The 10,000 ad impressions we get each day which try to convince us what shaving cream, what potato chip, what college, what mortgage rate, what charity, will make us happier.

- The monolith of the self-help industry. Whether it's "positive thinking" or "pain bodies" or the "law of attraction" or "optimism diets", none of that will ultimately work. Words are just words. Even this book won't do anything for anyone without hard practice and work. We want to be happy so we fork over our dollars to these industries. But at the end of the day we are all primarily householders. We don't have time to meditate for three hours and then do yoga and then do neurolinguistic programming and self-hypnosis while we diet.

We have families to raise. We have careers to pursue. We have money to make. We have colleagues and family to deal with. We have real fears that invade us at night. I have real fears. Things I'm scared of every single day. It's only through diligent work that we can start to overcome these fears. With fear comes stress, and stress leads to sickness, inertia, and all of the other things that slows down our happiness.

And sometimes we can't just wake up at 5:30am and go to sleep at 8 p.m. (as I suggest in my prior book) and write down 10 ideas a day. Sometimes we need to give ourselves a break and modify things until times and schedules permit. I'll discuss this more in part two by giving different exercises and modifications to the Daily Practice. How to deal with the people who bring us down, how to fight the fear, how to be creative – these are all components of bringing a daily practice into your life so that not only does your entire life change, it changes so quickly that you won't even recognize the final result.

KEEP IN TOUCH

Please join me on the Twitter Q&A sessions every Thursday at 3:30 p.m., or visit me at: jamesaltucher.com or Twitter.com/jaltucher.

Made in the USA
Lexington, KY
30 July 2013